Edward Eberstadt & Sons

Edward Eberstadt, 1883–1958.
Courtesy Yale Collection of Western Americana,
Beinecke Rare Book and Manuscript Library,
Yale University, New Haven, Connecticut.

Edward Eberstadt & Sons

❧

RARE BOOKSELLERS
OF WESTERN AMERICANA

MICHAEL VINSON

Foreword by
WILLIAM REESE

THE ARTHUR H. CLARK COMPANY
An imprint of the University of Oklahoma Press
Norman, Oklahoma
2016

LIBRARY OF CONGRESS CATALOGING-IN-PUBLICATION DATA

Name: Vinson, Michael, author.

Title: Edward Eberstadt & Sons : rare booksellers of Western Americana / Michael Vinson ; foreword by William Reese.

Description: Norman, Oklahoma : The Arthur H. Clark Company, an imprint of the University of Oklahoma Press, 2016. | Includes bibliographical references and index.

Identifiers: LCCN 2015049861 | ISBN 978-0-87062-438-4

Subjects: LCSH: Edward Eberstadt & Sons—History. | Antiquarian booksellers—New York (State)—New York—History—20th century. | West (U.S.)—History—Bibliography.

Classification: LCC Z473.E39 V56 2016 | DDC 381/.450020974710904—dc23

LC record available at http://lccn.loc.gov/2015049861

The paper in this book meets
the guidelines for permanence and durability of the
Committee on Production Guidelines for Book Longevity
of the Council on Library Resources, Inc. ∞

1 2 3 4 5 6 7 8 9 10

To my father,
THEODORE ALLEN VINSON
1933 ❧ 1962

Contents

Foreword

William Reese

For over half of the twentieth century, the rare book firm of Edward Eberstadt & Sons was the largest and most influential dealer in important books and manuscripts relating to the American West. From the founding of the firm by the young Edward Eberstadt in 1908 until its final disposal by his son Lindley in 1975, the two generations were important actors in the formation of collections, both private and public, in auctions, and in the discovery of previously buried sources in American history. While the firm is best remembered for selling western Americana, it might be most accurate to say it dealt in the history of the American frontier, as it progressed from east to west. Within those broad parameters Edward Eberstadt, and later his sons, not only made a handsome living but directly or indirectly helped build a spectrum of libraries and museums.

The secret history of great research libraries lies in the story of the rare book trade. These collections and institutions, quite reasonably, bear the names of the collectors who paid for them. Those names dot the pages of this book: Huntington, Wagner, Streeter, Coe, Beinecke, Graff, DeGolyer, and more. It takes nothing away from the talents and commitment of these men to look beneath the surface and explore how their great collections came into being. Some, such as Thomas W. Streeter, were deeply engaged as scholars with the printed material they collected. Others, such as William Robertson Coe, had a general idea of what they were collecting but left the details to others. In either case, the critical interlocutors in the translation of the raw material of history from attics, barns, and cupboards to reading rooms were the book and manuscript dealers who sought out the sources and brought them to the light of day.

The rare book trade of today has formidable research tools at its fingertips. Besides the obvious advantage of the Internet, there is a vast reference literature in the bibliography of American history: collection catalogues, specialized subject bibliographies, imprint bibliographies describing early printing, booksellers catalogues, exhibition listings, biographical dictionaries, scholarly editions of key works, and a vast secondary literature generated by generations of scholars. Virtually none of this existed when Edward Eberstadt entered the book trade in 1908. A successful antiquarian bookseller had to rely largely on memory and accumulated knowledge. The learning curve was steep, but the rewards for the active and attentive dealer were great; in time, few could match the depth and breadth of Eberstadt's knowledge of the literature in his chosen field. When it came to assertions of rarity or bibliographical detail, few could gainsay him. His retentive memory was his capital. Although diminished somewhat by the reference sources now available to anyone, the same is still true in the rare book trade today.

Edward Eberstadt, however, had two qualities that are also essential for any great antiquarian dealer, no matter what the subject area. The first is an intuitive sense of value—how an item might be priced. In order to price material to sell and make a profit, a dealer must buy at a lower price. There is no harder talent to acquire in any antique business, and it might fairly be equated with the use of the doubling cube in backgammon, compounding issues of strategy with questions of risk. Many people of great knowledge have failed as dealers because they did not understand this equation. The second quality, which Ed possessed to a remarkable degree, was an enthusiasm for his chosen area and a personality that conveyed it. He was a passionate man—in the depth of his love of his discipline, his warmth to his friends, and the vigor of his feuds. Like many others in the hard-living book trade of his time, he tempered his emotions with too much alcohol. While it certainly undermined his health, it never undercut his sunny, and by all accounts irresistible, demeanor. This was more than salesmanship; he was the business and the business was him.

The role of Lindley and Charles Eberstadt in the family firm was a critical one. Second-generation rare book firms are fairly common in Europe to this day, but most unusual in the United States. It is not clear if the two sons would have joined their father if the timing had been different, but graduating from college as they did in the depths of the Great Depression meant that jobs were hard to find, and their father needed their help. (Warren Howell, another leader of the trade, was forced to drop out of Stanford to help his father at John Howell–Books in San Francisco.) Whether it was initially by choice or necessity, the brothers took to the business with alacrity. They were perfect foils: Lindley was outgoing and personable, the salesman; Charles was shy and scholarly, the perfect researcher and cataloguer. Together the father and sons made a formidable team.

Even so, the Depression and World War II were a difficult period for even the most talented rare book dealers. While Edward's early career coincided with an almost uninterrupted boom time for rare books, the second half of his active days in the trade was a struggle for survival. By the time sunshine broke out again, with the spectacular rise of institutional collecting and the general prosperity of the 1950s, Edward was leaving the actual running of the firm to his sons. He was by then more the presiding genius of the firm than a daily participant. The collector of books on the western cattle trade, Jeff Dykes, recalled visiting in the early 1950s. As he walked past, Ed called out, "Hey, Jeff, come sit and talk for a while before my goddamn boys try to sell you something!" For Lindley and Charles, rare books was a business; for their father it was a way of life.

The later days of the firm were lucrative ones for Lindley and Charles. They capitalized on the many contacts and long relationships of the firm with collectors, institutions, and other dealers, while riding the wave of the boom in institutional collecting in the 1950s and '60s. They watched as many of the great private collections the firm had helped build were translated into public ones. The Eberstadts remained a major force in the Americana market through the fabulous Streeter Sale of 1966–69. After that the brothers were in slow retreat. Charles's death in 1974 led to the final sale of the business by Lindley in 1975.

Michael Vinson has done a valuable service in writing this book. He has dug beneath the surface and revealed something of the hidden history of the book trade as exemplified in one outstanding firm, and especially its remarkable founder, Edward Eberstadt.

Acknowledgments

I would like to thank George Miles, Coe Curator of Western Americana at the Beinecke Rare Book and Manuscript Library at Yale University—he went far above the call of duty in providing access to curatorial and other library files not normally open to the public. Megan von Ackermann read early drafts of this book and provided crucial support. William Reese is both a wonderful bookman and very helpful reader of the manuscript—this book is far better for his help. Nick Aretakis also provided some very helpful insights into the manuscript. My love for the Eberstadts was cultivated by Kansas bookman Michael Heaston, who kept a stack of Eberstadt catalogues on the toilet for perusing, and who first encouraged me to read and study their catalogues. David Farmer not only provided me with my first job and training in Western Americana, but also very helpfully lent me his stack of research correspondence on the collector Earl Vandale. Michael Ginsberg provided some helpful color and stories from his time helping John Jenkins to pack up the Eberstadt inventory. Gabriel Swift of the Princeton Collections of Western Americana provided quick and timely access to some crucial Philip Ashton Rollins correspondence for this book.

I would also like to thank the very helpful curatorial and reading room staffs of the Beinecke Rare Book and Manuscript Library and the archives of the Sterling Memorial Library at Yale University, New Haven, Connecticut; the American Antiquarian Society, Worcester, Massachusetts; the Newberry Library, Chicago, Illinois; the Denver Public Library, Denver, Colorado; the Western History Reading Room of the University of Oklahoma, Norman,

Oklahoma; the DeGolyer Library at Southern Methodist University, Dallas, Texas; the McCracken Research Library of the Buffalo Bill Center of the West, Cody, Wyoming; the Amon G. Carter Museum of American Art Archives, Fort Worth, Texas; and the Nita Stewart Haley Memorial Library, Midland, Texas. And finally, I would like to thank the very helpful editors and staff of the University of Oklahoma Press.

Edward Eberstadt & Sons

☙

1

Edward's Beginnings
to the Stock Market Crash
1908 ∻ 1929

An unlikely bookseller in New York City in the early 1900s almost single-handedly created a market among libraries and collectors for rare books about the American West. Edward Eberstadt was a maverick who combined the passion of a treasure hunter with the instincts of a scholar. The firm he established, Edward Eberstadt & Sons, eventually dominated the rare western American book market for nearly three-quarters of a century, from 1908 to 1975.[1]

The story of Eberstadt's beginning in the book trade combined serendipity with a savvy intuition—both of which would serve him well in the hunt for rare books. He had worked in western and South American gold mines for a couple of years but returned to New York by 1907. One day he was crossing the Brooklyn Bridge on foot when the urge to find a bathroom became pressing; reaching the Brooklyn side, he rushed into a garage and found the paper in the restroom was supplied by a stack of old books. Perusing them, he found one old volume in Spanish that piqued his interest, perhaps

---

[1]For more on Edward Eberstadt, see William Reese, "Pioneering in Western Americana," *AB Bookman's Yearbook* (Clifton, N.J.: AB Bookman's Weekly, 1985), 376–83; Jeff Dykes, "A Personal Memoir About Edward Eberstadt," *AB Bookman's Weekly* (October 7, 1985), 2512–13; William Reese, "Americana Booksellers," *The 1993 Pforzheimer Lecture of New York Public Library*, March 30, 1993, www.reeseco.com/pforz.htm (accessed August 6, 2014); Donald C. Dickinson, *Dictionary of American Antiquarian Bookdealers* (Westport, Conn.: Greenwood Press, 1998), 59–60; George L. Harding, "In Memoriam, Edward Emory Eberstadt," *California Historical Quarterly* 37 (December 1958), 375.

because of his Latin American experience. He purchased it from the garage owner for fifty cents and then took it to Wilberforce Eames, dean of Americana bibliographers at the New York Public Library,[2] who informed him that the book was a slightly imperfect early Mexican imprint, printed in the sixteenth century and very rare. Eberstadt sold it to an established New York rare book dealer, Lathrop Harper, and the one-time gold mine operator embarked on a new career searching for another type of treasure.[3]

Edward Eberstadt & Sons developed close relations with nearly every great collector of western books. Their customers included a number of institutions as well as private collectors such as Henry R. Wagner, a collector who compiled many western bibliographies and whose collections went to Yale, the Huntington Library, and other institutions; Everette L. DeGolyer, whose western rare book collection was eventually housed at Southern Methodist University in Dallas; Everett D. Graff, the Chicago businessman whose collection went to the Newberry Library in Chicago; William Robertson Coe, a New York businessman whose collection was given to Yale; and Thomas W. Streeter, the most famous collector of Americana of the twentieth century, whose collection was sold at auction. Those auction catalogues still comprise a major reference for western Americana. Many other prominent institutions and collectors benefited from the rare book expertise of the Eberstadt firm.

Edward Emory Eberstadt was born September 9, 1883, and after graduating from Mount Pleasant Military Academy in New York, he began his career working in gold mines in Idaho, California, and British Guiana. By 1907 he had returned to New York from British Guiana, where he married Anne Lindley of Louisville, Kentucky. His desire to remain closer to home with his new wife probably caused him to search out less adventurous opportunities. That same year he became one of the officers of a new periodical called *Tropical and Sub-Tropical America*, a Latin America travel magazine that lasted only one year.[4] Eberstadt's discovery of the Mexican rare book could not have come at a better time.

---

[2]Donald C. Dickinson, *Dictionary of American Book Collectors* (Westport, Conn.: Greenwood Press, 1986), 101–102.

[3]Lindley, Edward's son, later referred obliquely to this incident as his father entering the book business "by accident."

[4]You can see this magazine by going to Google Books and entering the title in the search box.

Inspired by his discovery of the early Mexican imprint, Eberstadt built on his Latin American experience (and presumably contacts) and began the Spanish American Book Company in 1907, which became the Latin-America Book Company in 1908.[5] Even in the early years of that first book business, some of his salesmanship was manifest. He was quick to prompt librarians when he did not receive an order after mailing out a list or catalogue. To Clarence Brigham, the librarian at the American Antiquarian Society, he wrote in 1910: "We haven't had any orders from you in a long while; from our lists, is there nothing of interest, or is it that the catalogues have not been received?"[6] It is probable that the paucity of interest in Latin America among American book buyers translated into a lack of orders, and eventually to a change in specialization for Eberstadt's book firm.

While his firm initially intended to specialize in "Modern, Rare and Antique" books from Latin America, it quickly became evident that many book collectors were only interested in the history of the American West. Perhaps the most prominent collector he met at this time was Henry R. Wagner, a mining engineer and executive of the Guggenheim family interests in copper mining and smelting.[7] Wagner's bibliographic works on the early Spanish Southwest and overland travel across the American West later became standards of bibliographic research.[8] Near the end of his life, Wagner wrote to Eberstadt of those early years: "I suppose you will recall that it is forty years or more since I first made your acquaintance, when you were flourishing under the name Latin American Book Company,"

---

[5]The American Antiquarian Society has four catalogues issued by the Latin-America Book Company (with a mimeograph list showing an address of 200 William Street, New York, and a rubber stamp on the same sheet "Removed to 118 East 26th"); two catalogues, numbers 5 and 6, have the address of 203 Front Street, New York; and one unnumbered catalogue is listed at 113th East 26th Street, New York.

[6]Edward Eberstadt to American Antiquarian Society, January 18, 1910. AAS Archives, American Antiquarian Society, Worcester, Mass.

[7]Dickinson, *Dictionary of American Book Collectors*, 324–25; Ruth Frey Axe, "Henry R. Wagner, An Intimate Profile," in *AB Bookman's Yearbook* (Clifton, N.J.: AB Bookman, 1979), 3; and Thomas W. Streeter, "Henry R. Wagner: Collector, Bibliographer, Cartographer, Historian," *California Historical Society Quarterly* 36 (June 1957), 165–75.

[8]Henry R. Wagner, *The Spanish Southwest, 1542–1794* (Albuquerque, N.M.: Quivira Society, 1937); Henry R. Wagner, *The Plains and the Rockies: A Bibliography of Original Narratives of Travel and Adventure, 1800–1865*, 4th ed., with additional editors Charles L. Camp and Robert H. Becker (San Francisco: John Howell–Books, 1982).

suggesting that they met about 1908.[9] Henry Wagner also noted in his memoirs that specializing in Latin America "was not a very lucrative business and Eberstadt shortly pushed into something that looked more promising, North Americana, and especially Western books. He had a supernatural knack of finding good books, which he still maintains in good working order."[10]

Some of Eberstadt's push into Western Americana is seen in catalogues 5 and 6 of the Latin-America Book Company, which had small sections relating to the history and exploration of the American West. These included a copy of Edward Smith's rare *An Account of a Journey through Northeastern Texas* (London, 1849), complete with the maps for $6.00, and a copy of the first edition of Josiah Gregg's *Commerce of the Prairies* (New York, 1844) a comparatively common book but described by Eberstadt as "A remarkable copy of the first edition, not shaken in the slightest, and with both text and plates almost as bright and fresh as if printed only a few months ago,"[11] only $13.50.[12]

Edward Eberstadt soon followed the western interests of his customers and decided to sell some of the inventory of the Latin-America Book Company at an auction of the Anderson Galleries in 1912.[13] He then reorganized under the name Hudson Book Company and began specializing in the American West.[14]

Who were the dealers in western American rare books when Eberstadt decided to specialize in this field in 1912? Certainly the leading dealer in Americana was Lathrop Harper, who began in 1891 with his brother Francis; they also published important and scholarly editions

---

[9]Henry R. Wagner to Edward Eberstadt, May 6, 1949. Box 1, Henry Raup Wagner Papers, Beinecke Library, Yale University.

[10]Henry R. Wagner, *Bullion to Books: Fifty Years of Business and Pleasure* (Los Angeles: Zamarano Club, 1942), 201–202.

[11]*Latin-America Book Company*, Catalogue 5: 756 (American Antiquarian Society copy).

[12]As of 2015, the Smith book on Texas brings around $5,000 and the Josiah Gregg around $6,000.

[13]Interestingly, much of the Latin American inventory was still being stored in 1975 and was acquired by the Jenkins Company as part of their purchase.

[14]The Hudson Book Company was at 862 Hewitt Place in the Bronx in 1913, and by 1918 he was operating at 25 West 42nd Street, New York, and then by 1920 or so at 47–65 West 42nd Street—which later was listed as 55 West 42nd Street. One of the unanswered questions about the Hudson Book Company is whether Eberstadt had a silent partner who invested in his business; that the company records have not survived means the question is unanswerable for now.

of the journals of Lewis and Clark and others. Harper specialized not only in rare books of America but was also the leading dealer in incunabula (European books printed before 1500). He had risen to such prominence that when the *New York Herald* did a cartoon featuring the dealers fighting over the rarities at the Robert Hoe Sale in 1912, Harper's caricature was featured alongside those of George D. Smith (the New York rare book dealer who was Henry Huntington's agent) and Dr. A. S. W. Rosenbach (considered the most important American rare book dealer of the first half of the twentieth-century). Harper was also the chief Americana dealer for the Michigan collector William L. Clements. It was to Eberstadt's advantage in business to develop a close working relationship—which eventually became a close friendship—with Lathrop Harper.[15]

Some other New York dealers dealt in western Americana but were not specialists in the West, as they also handled all periods of American history. Adolph Stager and Charles P. Everitt were partners in the Cadmus Bookshop in New York from 1910 to 1928 and dealt in Americana. Everitt later became known for rare western Americana.[16] David Kirschenbaum of the Carnegie Book Shop in New York also specialized in Americana and was beginning around the same time as Eberstadt. (Eventually H. Bradley Martin, scion of a wealthy New York family, became one of his best customers for Americana.)[17] Another antiquarian bookseller who came to prominence about this time was Michael Walsh of Goodspeed's Bookshop in Boston, who the head of its Americana department in 1915; over the years he would uncover many western rarities.[18]

[15]Harper was also apparently a regular at Eberstadt's Saturday bridge games (as were several other book dealers). For more on Harper, see Donald C. Dickinson, *Dictionary of American Antiquarian Bookdealers* (Westport, Conn.: Greenwood Press, 1998), 92–93; Thomas R. Adams, "Lathrop Colgate Harper, 1867–1950," *Gazette of the Grolier Club* 26/27 (1977), 3–22; Charles F. Heartman, "Lathrop Colgate Harper," *The American Collector* 1 (January 1926), 139–43; Lawrence C. Wroth, "Lathrop Colgate Harper, A Happy Memory," *Papers of the Bibliographical Society of America* 52 (1958), 161–72; "Lathrop C. Harper, Book Dealer, Dead," *New York Times*, August 13, 1950, 42.

[16]Dickinson, *Dictionary of American Antiquarian Bookdealers*, 209 for Stager; 63–64 for Everitt. See especially Charles P. Everitt, *Adventures of a Treasure Hunter* (Boston: Little, Brown, 1951), for a delightful read about his adventures.

[17]Dickinson, *Dictionary of American Antiquarian Bookdealers*, 110–11.

[18]Dickinson, *Dictionary of American Antiquarian Bookdealers*, 223–24. Another New York dealer who later became important in western Americana, Peter Decker, did not issue his first catalogue until 1938.

In the midst of these Americana dealers, Edward Eberstadt seems to have been the earliest to pioneer the specialty of the American West. One of his early Hudson Book Company catalogues was titled "Americana" and issued in three parts. The initial reaction to part 1 was so welcome that Eberstadt printed the remarks of a couple of collectors on the cover wrappers of part 2. The Rev. Nathaniel S. Thomas, Episcopal bishop of Wyoming and a western book collector who played a major role in Eberstadt's early career, said, "The most remarkable collection of books in any one catalogue, relating to the Western states, that I have ever seen."[19] L. Bradford Prince, president of the Historical Society of New Mexico, said, "I must compliment you on your remarkable collection of works on the Southwest."[20] These were nice endorsements for any bookseller's catalogue from two well-known collectors.

One significant pair of catalogues from the Hudson Book Company at this time demonstrates why the Eberstadt listings would later become reference works: *How They Went West! Pioneer Narratives of the Overland Trail* (which was 12 pages long with 77 items) and *When the West was New! Source Books of the "Wild & Wooley": Being the Second Part of My "How They Went West" Catalogue* (23 pages and 100 items). Both catalogues were unnumbered, suggesting that Eberstadt may have had a specific customer in mind for the catalogues. In both, the entry for each book includes a lengthy description of its importance and bibliography, instead of just the usual listing of title and price for this time.[21]

Eberstadt's specialization in western America was taken to an exciting new level in 1920 when he met his most important customer for the next three decades, William Robertson Coe of Oyster Bay, Long Island.[22] Coe, an executive with the marine insurance firm of Johnson & Higgins, became even richer through his marriage to the daughter of Henry H. ("Hell-Hound") Rogers, one of John D.

---

[19]*Hudson Book Company*, Catalogue 27, "Americana: Part II" (American Antiquarian Society copy), blurb on front cover wrapper.

[20]Ibid.

[21]These two Hudson Book Company catalogues are unnumbered, but copies are in the American Antiquarian Society bookseller catalogue collection.

[22]Dickinson, *Dictionary of American Book Collectors*, 72–73; Edward Eberstadt, "The William Robertson Coe Collection of Western Americana," *Yale Library Gazette* 23 (October 1948), 1–130.

Rockefeller's chief henchmen in the Standard Oil empire. In 1909 Coe purchased Buffalo Bill's Irma Ranch in Cody, Wyoming, as a hunting retreat. Here he met the Wyoming book collector Rev. Nathaniel Thomas and first developed an interest in collecting rare western books.

There are two stories about how Coe met Edward Eberstadt. One is preserved in oral tradition, and the other is documented in the archives; the truth probably lies in a combination of the two accounts. Around 1920, Bishop Thomas, an admirer of the Eberstadt catalogues, was "worn thin in the quest" (Coe's phrase) with collecting western books and recommended that Coe get in touch with Edward Eberstadt to help him build a collection of rare western books.[23] Coe was not a beginning collector—he had already cultivated and collected rare orchids at his Oyster Bay estate (today a museum and horticultural center, "Planting Fields") and had invested substantial sums in prize racehorses as well. He may not have known much about rare books at the beginning, but he knew how to judge people.

Part of what may have worn Bishop Thomas thin in his collecting quest was the avariciousness of a fierce competitor, Henry Wagner. As Eberstadt recounted later: "In actuality, the Bishop was responsible for my first meeting with Mr. Coe and as he told me he was motivated by a desire to get even with one Henry R. Wagner. He said he was sick and tired of having Wagner grab off all the Western treasures that came into the market and desired once and for all to choke him off by inducing Mr. Coe to enter the field."[24]

Perhaps Wagner had hoped, as many collectors fantasize occasionally, that he could intimidate other competitors into submission. If so, that strategy backfired when Bishop Thomas brought Coe into the western book collecting game. Eberstadt wrote to Thomas: "Well Bishop I thank you for recommending me to Mr. Coe & I do hope he will give me the opportunity he spoke of—building him up a collection—if he does—I will do my best for him."[25]

---

[23]W. R. Coe, "Memorandum," Box 10, Edward Eberstadt & Sons Records, Beinecke Library, Yale University.

[24]Edward Eberstadt to James T. Babb, November 16, 1948. Box 35, University Library, Manuscripts and Archives, Yale University Library.

[25]Edward Eberstadt to Bishop Nathaniel Thomas, May 10, 1920. Box 8, Eberstadt Records, Beinecke Library.

Of course, in a small collecting world like that of rare books, Wagner soon heard about Coe, but he was inclined at first to discount the new collector's importance to the market, insisting that rising prices were just standard Eberstadt practice: "All this talk of Eberstadt keeping books for Coe is bunk. If he finds out you are looking for railroad pamphlets or any other kind, you will have to pay three or four times what they are worth. He finds books, all right, but you have to have unlimited means to deal with him nowadays."[26] Wagner did not want to believe that a collector of comparatively unlimited wealth would become a factor in the rare book game.

The other version of how Eberstadt met Coe may have been Bishop Thomas's recommendation that Coe visit Eberstadt's store in New York City (at that time at 25 West 42nd Street, opposite the New York Public Library). The story goes that Eberstadt was playing his weekly Saturday-afternoon bridge game with bookseller friends in the back room when a gentleman wandered in and started browsing around. Anyone who has worked in a bookstore well knows how many people come in to kill a few minutes and just browse—the vast majority leave without a purchase. This customer was different. Eventually Coe must have found the card players in the back of the store and asked about the sections in which he would have been most interested—Wyoming and the Pacific Northwest. Edward might have gotten up from the game, gestured to a few sections of the store, and returned to the table. Perhaps curiosity got the best of him; in any event, sometime later something took him to the front of the store, where he found that the stranger had several large stacks of books on the front counter ready to purchase. According to legend, Eberstadt turned on his heel, went to the back room, and said, "Sorry, boys, the game's over," and waved them away. They took the hint and disappeared while Eberstadt helped his new customer—probably also taking the opportunity to discourse at some length on the books as well.[27]

Another collector who encountered the weekly card game during two visits to Eberstadt's store in 1927 was Everett Graff, president

[26]Henry R. Wagner to Thomas W. Streeter, September 3, 1928. Box 14, Thomas W. Streeter Papers, American Antiquarian Society, Worcester, Mass.

[27]As related by Lindley Eberstadt to William Reese; see William S. Reese, "Americana Booksellers," *The 1993 Pforzheimer Lecture.*

of Ryerson Steel and patron of cultural institutions in Chicago.[28] These visits evidently made a good impression, and both men seemed sincere in their desire to connect. Eberstadt wrote Graff about the game: "Well, as I predicted I got sandbagged in the card game Saturday, and I only hope that you had better luck on the way home and found an easier gang to play bridge with than were the bunch of sharks I played host to."[29] This visit was the beginning of a great customer relationship and later long-standing friendship.

Another customer recalled that Eberstadt loved to talk on about the West and western books, and it probably only took a slightly eager ear to bring him out. Everette L. DeGolyer lived in New York and was president of Amerada Petroleum (later he moved to Dallas as a partner in the geophysical exploration firm of DeGolyer-McNaughton). After he dropped by the store in 1928, Eberstadt wrote, "I must say that I enjoyed your visit immensely and had a lovely time talking about myself to an entirely new pair of ears. Thanks a thousand times for the opportunity. Assuming that I didn't bore you stiff, I am going to ask you to please come up again real soon, and if you will do so, I promise to put a clothespin on my mouth and devote part of the time at least to showing you a few books. It occurred to me after you left that perhaps you came to look at books rather than to listen to one of my monologues."[30]

Regardless of Eberstadt's claim of talking about himself instead of showing DeGolyer books, Everette purchased some important books at that visit in 1928—including Joseph McCoy, *Historic Sketches of the Cattle Trade* (Kansas City, 1874), $22.50; Capt. John Mullan, *Miners and Travelers' Guide to Oregon, Washington, Idaho, Montana, Wyoming and Colorado* (New York, 1865), $8.50; and the very rare Zenas Leonard, *Narrative of the Adventures of Zenas Leonard* (Clearfield, Penn., 1839)—about one of the earliest fur trade

---

[28]Dickinson, *Dictionary of American Book Collectors*, 141–42; also the informative study by John Blew, *The Lives and Work of Wright and Zoe Howes and the Story of U.S.iana* (Chicago: Privately printed, 2014), which includes much information on Graff; and Colton Storm, *A Catalogue of the Everett D. Graff Collection of Western Americana* (Chicago: Published for the Newberry Library by the University of Chicago Press, 1968), v–vi.

[29]Edward Eberstadt to Everett D. Graff, May 23, 1927. Box 4, Folder 3, Edward D. Graff Papers, Newberry Library, Chicago.

[30]Edward Eberstadt to Everette L. DeGolyer, November 1, 1928. DeGolyer Library, Southern Methodist University, Dallas, Texas.

expeditions to California—for $350. This last purchase was a good buy at the time, since another copy of the Leonard had sold at auction the year before in the Braislin Sale for $720.[31]

Eberstadt's first visit with Coe in the store was apparently a successful encounter, but the addition of such a major customer made other demands on his rare book business. Coe insisted that the bookseller enter the twentieth century and get a telephone for his business so that Coe could call him when he desired. This was not as easy, cheap, or self-evident as we might think now. The first U.S. transcontinental telephone line was only finished in 1914, and long-distance calls typically took operators at each end around seven minutes to set up and connect the parties.[32] In the early 1920s in New York, business calls were sold in local monthly contracts that averaged around ten cents per call; while this may not seem onerous today, it meant a cost of around two dollars per local call at the time, with steep additional charges for long distance.

At one point Eberstadt playfully scribbled at the top of his new letterhead (changing the name from Hudson Book Company to Edward Eberstadt in January 1921, though the catalogues retained the Hudson name for a couple more years), "And next I'll get a telephone!"[33] Then just over a month later he wrote Coe, "Well I have finally arranged to have that telephone put in, which you *demand*. I bought another chap's contract paying a bonus of $50 for it. Now, I should have the instrument ready to talk through in a week or ten days."[34]

Even though Eberstadt complied with Coe's demand that he install a telephone, their relationship was often prickly, particularly in regard to the prices of rare books. The most important aspects of Eberstadt's business were ones that are important to all antiquarian booksellers: what to price your wares at, and how to describe and place them in a context that justifies the price.

---

[31]In today's dollars, the McCoy would be around $4,000, the Mullan guide around $2,000, and the last copy of the Zenas Leonard at auction (February 2015) brought $125,000.

[32]Anonymous, "History: Long Distance Telephone," *Cybertelecom*, www.cybertelecom .org/notes/long_distance.htm (accessed August 7, 2014).

[33]Edward Eberstadt to W. R. Coe, January 10, 1921. Box 8, Eberstadt Records, Beinecke Library.

[34]Edward Eberstadt to W. R. Coe, March 18, 1921. Box 8, Eberstadt Records, Beinecke Library.

Bishop Thomas may have wondered what he had started once Coe began to compete against him for Wyoming books. Perhaps he thought Coe was pushing prices higher for books that the bishop would have liked to buy; in any event, he apparently told Coe he was paying too much. While Coe was a very wealthy and successful businessman, he did not get rich by unnecessarily spending money, and this conversation about book prices with Thomas must have disturbed him. Coe wrote to Eberstadt, "I saw Bishop Thomas yesterday. He thinks I am paying high prices for books."[35]

Apparently Coe did not receive a response to this little jab about prices, and just a couple of weeks later he wrote again to Eberstadt: "In this connection, I want to have a more definite understanding with you. . . . Considering the number of purchases you are making for me, I am not satisfied with the high percentage of profit you are taking. If I am to continue having you buy books for me on such a large scale, we must have a clearer understanding regarding this."[36] Any bookseller acting as an agent for a wealthy collector must tread with care, particularly if the customer begins to feel that the bookseller is taking advantage of them.

Early in the twentieth century, the prominent New York City bookseller George D. Smith was the book-buying agent for the California railroad magnate Henry Huntington, whose estate is now a museum, research library, and botanical garden in San Marino, California. Smith once remarked to fellow bookseller Charlie Everitt that "Charlie, you're absolutely crazy. You deal every day with men who think in thousands, and you talk in five dollar bills."[37] Everitt remarked that Smith never made that mistake in dealing with wealthy clients. Reportedly Huntington, when told that Smith was overcharging him, simply replied, "Well, he got me the books, didn't he?"

George Smith may have had his mogul Huntington—a collector who thought in "thousand dollar bills"—but while Eberstadt's Coe was wealthy, he was also concerned about how much he was paying

---

[35]W. R. Coe to Edward Eberstadt, June 11, 1920. Box 8, Eberstadt Records, Beinecke Library.

[36]W. R. Coe to Edward Eberstadt, June 23, 1920. Box 8, Eberstadt Records, Beinecke Library.

[37]Everitt, *Adventures of a Treasure Hunter*, 187.

for rare books. Later that fall Coe wrote Eberstadt: "The more I think of the way I am buying books from you the more I become convinced that it is resulting in a serious rise in prices and that I am paying you inordinate profits."[38] Almost every major collector at some point comes to believe that they alone are driving up the prices in the antiquarian book market.

Coe continued complaining:

> This is particularly so of the more ordinary material which so frequently shows up in catalogues. The seven items which I got from Goodspeed's [a leading Boston antiquarian bookseller] cost $34.25 and from my examination of similar purchases from you I am convinced that if you had these they would have cost me three times that amount. In the past few months I have been dealing with you I have bought over $13,000 worth of books from you and I have told you on numerous occasions that on stuff which you acquired I felt that a profit of 40% was all you should expect when you had such large dealings with me. . . .[39] I have acquired the feeling that you have made inordinate profits on what you have sold me. . . . I have about made up my mind I shall not continue to purchase from you on the present basis and there must be a showdown on every item as to what it has cost you.[40]

Some of Coe's concern about Eberstadt's prices may have come from his own scouting experience. Every collector, of course, wants to take part in the book collecting treasure hunt and find his own gems—and bargains—as well. At one point Coe dropped in on an unidentified bookstore and bought a small pamphlet guide to the Montana gold rush: "I picked up for a song a little pamphlet I had never seen before nor remember it in Wagner. . . . Look it up and tell me if it is any good, perhaps I may have it. I hope not as I like its looks and also like to pick up a nice item on my own."[41] Coe had great scouting instincts—that little pamphlet he discovered and

---

[38]W. R. Coe to Edward Eberstadt, October 8, 1920. Box 8, Eberstadt Records, Beinecke Library.

[39]$13,000 in 1920 was an enormous sum of money; perhaps something close to $250,000 today.

[40]W. R. Coe to Edward Eberstadt, October 8, 1920. Box 8, Eberstadt Records, Beinecke Library.

[41]W. R. Coe to Edward Eberstadt, May 9, 1922. Box 8, Eberstadt Records, Beinecke Library. The pamphlet was titled *Thompson's Complete Guide to the New Gold Regions of Upper Missouri, Deer Lodge, Beaver Head, Nez Perce, Salmon River, Boise River, Powder River, John Day, . . .* (St. Louis, 1863).

"purchased for a song" was Charles Whittlesey's *Mineral Resources* (Cleveland, 1863), a rare guide to the Montana gold rush. In the nearly one hundred years since he found that copy, only one other copy has appeared in the antiquarian market.[42]

Eberstadt, like any good antiquarian bookseller, parried by pointing out the remarkable purchases Coe had made from him. In December of that year, Eberstadt thanked Coe for his patronage and wrote: "My efforts have not resulted in your acquiring a collection of rare books cheaply—but I have done everything possible to *get you the books*—and a survey of the results is pleasing to me (and I hope too, to yourself) for I know of no collector who has acquired the material you now possess and many of them [you] have had for years—Wyeth—Pattie, Leonard, Maximilian, Lewis Portfolio, Palmer, Dimsdale, Campbell Idaho—These are not things one can place a value on, it might be a decade ere another of any of them comes to light, so I close, hoping you have found your book hunter a good digger."[43]

In other words, even if the job was not done cheaply, at least it was done well—and, after all, as Eberstadt pointed out, Coe now owned the rare books. The eight books that Eberstadt listed to remind Coe are among the great rarities of any western collection: John Wyeth's *Oregon* (1833; the first printed account of an emigrant journey across the plains); James Pattie's *Personal Narrative* (presumably the very rare 1831 edition and not the 1833 with the reprinted title page); Zenas Leonard's *Narrative* (1839); Prince Maximilian's *Travels in the Interior of North America* (1839–41), with the great aquatint engravings by Karl Bodmer; James O. Lewis's *Aboriginal Portfolio* (Philadelphia, 1835–36); Joel Palmer's *Journal of Travels over the Rocky Mountains* (Cincinnati, 1847); Thomas Dimsdale's *The Vigilantes of Montana* (Virginia City, Montana Territory, 1866); and John Campbell's rare miner's guide, *Idaho: Six Months in the Gold Diggings* (Chicago, 1864).

Eberstadt was also willing to take a poke at himself about prices, even in those early years when Coe was poking him plenty: "In this same mail I have received the Cadmus catalogue and noted therein

---

[42]This guide is number 396 in Wagner's bibliography of overland travel and guidebooks, *The Plains and the Rockies*. Ernest Wessen of Midland Rare Book Company had a copy in his catalogue 70 in 1958.

[43]Edward Eberstadt to W. R. Coe, undated but circa December 1920. Box 8, Eberstadt Records, Beinecke Library.

the copy of Matthews [*sic*] 'Colorado.'"[44] Mathews's *Pencil Sketches of Colorado* is one of the great lithographic view books of the trans-Mississippi West. Eberstadt continued, tongue in cheek: "This is priced at $500. I have not looked up our cost on this, but if memory serves me, we saved $400 on this work. Can it be that I am getting to be a back number, and don't know what to charge? Do I hear you saying, 'Not on your life Eberstadt'?"[45]

The Americana collector (and prominent banker) Thomas W. Streeter was fond of Edward Eberstadt and did not mind the occasional overpriced book. He once wrote back to Wagner in defense of his bookseller friend: "I haven't seen our mutual friend Eberstadt for four or five weeks. . . . I know that he does rob me from time to time, but he does it so gracefully and nicely that I don't mind very much."[46] Streeter continued with a description of the one part of the dealer-collector relationship that was very important to him. "You can always rely on Eberstadt to take back at any time a book you have bought from him if you happen to find a better copy somewhere else or if you pick up a copy a good deal cheaper somewhere else."

Streeter continued by recounting an example of this: "Some months ago I got from Eberstadt the Shoemaker Report of the Preliminary Surveys of the Union Pacific from Fort Riley to Denver City, with maps. It had a crazy auction record of three or four hundred dollars and I paid him $135 for it. His copy lacked the wrappers and the maps were mounted on linen. This summer I picked up in Cincinnati a beautiful copy in the original wrappers with the maps as issued, for $20, and Eberstadt didn't have the slightest hesitation in taking back the copy he got from me."[47] For Streeter, dealing

---

[44]Edward Eberstadt to W. R. Coe, October 9, 1926. Box 8, Eberstadt Records, Beinecke Library.

[45]Edward Eberstadt to W. R. Coe, October 9, 1926. Box 8, Eberstadt Records, Beinecke Library.

[46]Thomas W. Streeter to Henry R. Wagner, September 19, 1928. Box 14, Folder 1, Streeter Papers, American Antiquarian Society. For more on Streeter, see also Dickinson, *Dictionary of American Book Collectors*, 301–303; Edward Eberstadt, "The Thomas W. Streeter Collection," *Yale Library Gazette* 31 (April 1957), 147–53; Frank Streeter, "Some Recollections of Thomas W. Streeter and His Collecting," *Gazette of the Grolier Club* 32 (1980), 40–50; and two catalogues of the William Reese Company, *128 The Streeter Sale Revisited* (New Haven, Conn., 1993) and *257 The Streeter Sale Revisited* (New Haven, Conn., 2007), each with an introduction and thoughts about Streeter and his collection by William Reese.

[47]Thomas W. Streeter to Henry R. Wagner, September 19, 1928. Box 14, Folder 1, Streeter Papers, American Antiquarian Society.

with a reputable dealer who will stand behind his wares was worth something, even if the prices were higher.

Although Coe was his most valuable customer, Eberstadt met another new collector in the 1920s though Bishop Thomas. Charles B. Voorhis was a bank president in Wisconsin who had purchased a ranch in Wyoming, and he became acquainted with Thomas because of their shared enthusiasm for western history. Sometime in the fall of 1924 the bishop was visiting Eberstadt, who afterward wrote to Voorhis:

> Bishop Thomas has just been in to see me. Somehow, despite my many sins—or perhaps, because of them—the Bishop honors us with a little visit whenever he chances to wend eastward, and on this occasion, during our chat, he told me of you and your interest in Western books. The Bishop selected several items which he suggested as belonging in your collection, and took with him some of our recent catalogues which he will himself send to you. In the meantime, pending your perusal of these lists, we are forwarding to you for your approval and examination the volumes already suggested."[48]

What is most striking about this exchange is the sending of a package of books on approval without even asking the customer first (much less getting paid first), but it is evident from their correspondence that the Eberstadts did this a number of times with newer customers. Eberstadt not only built trust with new collectors this way, but he also probably knew that a book in hand is easier to sell than only a description in a quote. The books arrived a few days later, and Voorhis wrote to Eberstadt thanking him and asking if he had the edition of Lewis and Clark edited by Rueben G. Thwaites (Dodd, Mead, 1905). Another beginning collector was lured into the Eberstadt fold.

Eberstadt responded to Voorhis with some advice for the novice collector in his next letter: "The bringing together of a representative collection of Wyoming is not an easy feat, nor can it be done wholesale—it requires vigilance, patience, and time—lots of all three, but as the years pass and the library grows, each new possession means an ache satisfied, an ambition achieved—this after all is as near, I believe, as we ever get to happiness. And thrills!"[49] With this letter

---

[48]Hudson Book Company to Charles B. Voorhis, October 22, 1924. William Reese, Private Collection.

[49]Edward Eberstadt to Charles B. Voorhis, November 10, 1924. William Reese, Private Collection.

he shipped some more books on approval to Voorhis, including a book of Wyoming laws that he touted as the "first book printed in Wyoming" (actually now believed to be printed in Chicago).[50]

Voorhis thought on receipt of the books that he should explain his collecting desires in a little more detail to Eberstadt: "As you know, I became interested in Wyoming history because of the fact that I have a ranch out there and spend quite a little time in the upper Wind River Valley, about ninety miles from Lander, each summer."[51] The Wind River is a beautiful little valley in western Wyoming and was the location of several fur trade rendezvous on the Green River in the 1830s. Perhaps if Eberstadt had realized the fur trade rendezvous connection—particularly with the Green River's location in the Wind River valley—he might have been able to steer Voorhis's collecting in that direction too.

Eberstadt's way with words was not the only thing that drew collectors such as Voorhis into his firm; he was able to tempt them with real treasures. He brought Thomas Dimsdale's *Vigilantes of Montana* (Virginia City, Montana Territory, 1866), the first book printed in Montana, to Voorhis's attention. This book was often touted with the claim that Charles Dickens called it "the most interesting book I ever read." While this statement is undocumented, what Dickens actually wrote to a book reviewer in 1868 about the Dimsdale (a copy of which was in his library at his death) was, "Your account of the Vigilance book is a most admirable presentation and condensation of a wandering text."[52] This was hardly a ringing endorsement by the famous author, but the rare book trade rewrote it to help sell the book.

The Dimsdale book certainly whetted the collecting passions of Voorhis. He had visited Bishop Thomas again, and seeing the Dimsdale book, wrote Eberstadt asking for one, who replied:

I have now located a most interesting copy of this work—it is N. P. Langford's own copy, who was a famous explorer and author of his

---

[50]The book was *General Laws, Memorials and Resolutions of the Territory of Wyoming* (Chicago?, 1870). As Thomas W. Streeter notes in his entry for this book in Streeter Sale IV: 2235: "This compilation was for some time considered the first book printed in Wyoming; it is certainly the earliest official book printing"; now it is thought to be a Chicago imprint.

[51]Charles B. Voorhis to Edward Eberstadt, November 17, 1924. William Reese, Private Collection.

[52]Charles Dickens to Henry Morley, June 11, 1868, in *The Letters of Charles Dickens* (New York: Oxford University Press, 2002), 131.

own book on Montana history, *Vigilante Days and Ways* (Boston, 1890) and contains his book label on the inside front cover. I may say, in passing, that when I was in Helena some two years ago for Mr. Coe, Mr. Saunders, then Librarian of the State Library held his copy at $1000—I do not subscribe to this valuation, but I have to admit that I know of no other copy which it would now be possible to buy at any price whatsoever. I valued the book in one of my old lists at $150 and should have received a subsidy from the telegraph office on account of the wires it occasioned. That copy is now at Harvard University. I am attempting to secure this so as to be able to sell it at $250—I may have to go a bit higher, but am a fair poker player when it comes to books. It is one of the greatest of western literary nuggets, and while I am not going to let it get away, I can gain nothing by rushing the purchase.[53]

Voorhis was delighted with this news but warned Eberstadt not to disclose the price to anyone lest he be "examined for my sanity."[54] Just a couple of weeks later Eberstadt was able to report the good news to Voorhis:

I have great pleasure in reporting that I have today concluded the purchase of the original edition of Dimsdale's *Vigilantes of Montana*, (1866). The volume goes forward by express today and should reach you not later than Wednesday. While there are books on the west which cost more than Dimsdale, I know of few inherently more rare, and practically none which, were I limited to choice, I would rather own. Good wine needs no bush, but I am very anxious that you appreciate the rarity of this little volume and the extreme good fortune which is ours in its acquisition.[55]

Later Eberstadt summarized Voorhis's reaction on receiving the Dimsdale: "Your confession of a thrill of pride of ownership, warms me all over and I exult with you in its successful acquisition. Heaven help the next man who sets his heart on obtaining a copy."[56]

Voorhis loved the Dimsdale but was still concerned with how the Wyoming book of laws would fit into his collection. "I am not so sure of the volume, *First Laws of Wyoming*. Laws are uninteresting except to the real student and I suspect that there are a number of these volumes in existence and my first feeling is that except for the fact, as you

---

[53]Edward Eberstadt to Charles B. Voorhis, April 15, 1925. William Reese, Private Collection.
[54]Charles B. Voorhis to Edward Eberstadt, April 17, 1925. William Reese, Private Collection.
[55]Edward Eberstadt to Charles B. Voorhis, April 25, 1925. William Reese, Private Collection.
[56]Edward Eberstadt to Charles B. Voorhis, May 5, 1925. William Reese, Private Collection.

say, that it is the first book published in Wyoming, that it would be valuable or interesting only as a book of reference."[57] Many booksellers have discovered since then that any attempt to sell law books to collectors of history will be met with almost universal lack of interest.

Eberstadt, however, refused to surrender any ground on the Wyoming law book; it was rare, and the collector should keep it—and perhaps also the fact that law books were slow to sell fueled his enthusiasm. This salesmanship for the Wyoming book of laws would manifest itself in the Eberstadt catalogues, where it kept reappearing like a dandelion on an otherwise verdant lawn.

Eberstadt admonished the new collector: "With regard to the Wyoming Laws—I must, if you will permit me to do so, most strongly urge that it be retained in the collection. It is the first volume printed in the Territory and as such, if for no other reason—and there are more than several—should in my opinion most certainly fill a niche in the library you are creating." Eberstadt was willing to concede that the volume "does not look 'rare,'" but insisted the lack of it down the road in Voorhis's library would be a "grievous mistake." Then, perhaps worried that he might have poured it on a little thick about the law book, Eberstadt asked that Voorhis not regard his discussion as mere "sales talk."[58]

Eberstadt was successful; Voorhis wrote him, "I am going to take your advice and will keep the copy of Wyoming laws."[59] Eberstadt was more than pleased that his exertion resulted in a sale, and wrote tongue in cheek: "I noted with special pleasure that you have decided to keep the Wyoming laws. Someday in the future—when the Western collection has taken more definite form—I shall not be surprised to hear that you have called your board together to decide on a memorial tablet to be erected in my honor for so persistently urging this purchase."[60] If the tablet in Eberstadt's honor was not erected by Voorhis, it certainly should be by every antiquarian bookseller who has ever tried to sell a law book to a customer.

[57]Charles B. Voorhis to Edward Eberstadt, November 17, 1924. William Reese, Private Collection.

[58]Edward Eberstadt to Charles B. Voorhis, December 2, 1924. William Reese, Private Collection.

[59]Charles B. Voorhis to Edward Eberstadt, December 11, 1924. William Reese, Private Collection.

[60]Edward Eberstadt to Charles B. Voorhis, December 16, 1924. William Reese, Private Collection.

Eberstadt was also imaginative and sometimes thought of amazing ways to overcome price objections; after his death, James Babb recounted the following anecdote:

> One of his best clients from San Francisco made two trips yearly to New York in the early Twenties. Ed would have a good collection of rare and important material laid out for him. Invariably the client would take everything but always with the bored statement, after tossing the rare pamphlets to one side, "these are alright, but can't you turn up something really exciting?" This finally got under Ed's skin, so on the latest visit he did have something exciting, a broadside— a Zamorano imprint—the first one, I believe, of the first printer in California. This was one of two or three known copies. In preparation for the visit Ed went to his bank and borrowed a $10,000 Liberty Bond. He placed the bond and the folded up imprint in his coat pocket. After looking at all of the books on the table, the client came out with his regular remark quoted above. Ed said, "Yes, I have something really exciting" and whipped out the broadside and explained it. The client for a second forgot himself and said, "That IS exciting." Immediately realizing his mistake he sobered up and casually asked the price. Ed said, "$10,000." The client was shocked and shaken at such a price for a mere piece of paper with a little printing on one side and said so. Ed then whipped out the Liberty Bond and asked the client, "How many of these do you have in your bank?" The reply was "Thousands. Why do you ask?" Ed then turned to the Zamorano and said, "And how many of these do you have?" The sale was consummated.[61]

In Eberstadt's efforts to convince his customers of the importance of a book to their collections, he was always a little sensitive about being called a salesman. In this regard Eberstadt once wrote to Voorhis about his finding of the rare Charles Wilkes, *Narrative of the United States Exploring Expedition* (Philadelphia, 1844): "I have secured a very beautiful copy of Wilkes' Narrative, but as you might again accuse me of salesmanship if I were to write about it at the end of this letter I won't say a word this time." But of course Eberstadt was unable to restrain himself and added, "But jiminy, it's a wonder!"[62] Voorhis, of course, could not let this "saintly bit of

---

[61]James T. Babb to Sol M. Malkin, November 5, 1958, Box 27, Manuscripts and Archives, Yale University Library.

[62]Edward Eberstadt to Charles B. Voorhis, May 26, 1925. William Reese, Private Collection.

dessert" pass and asked to know more about the Wilkes narrative.[63] It is remarkable that Eberstadt always knew just the right amount of bait to dangle before the collector.

Nevertheless, a large pocketbook did not always mean a ready sale—no matter how much a bookseller may love a book. And for Eberstadt, this could be some degree of love. Early in 1921 he offered to Coe the very rare Eleazer Ingalls overland guide, *Journal of a Trip to California across the Plains in 1850–51* (Waukegan, Ill., 1852) with the author's original manuscript of the guidebook as well. Apparently Coe was reluctant to plunge, probably because the book fell outside of his primary area of interest: the Pacific Northwest. This lack of interest did not deter Eberstadt, who wrote: "In the event you do not purchase the Ingalls—please let me have the 'copy' tomorrow, so I can put it with the original and show Mr. Crocker."[64] Templeton Crocker of San Francisco was building an important collection of Californiana, and Eberstadt's invocation of a rival collector's name was intended as a prod to Coe.[65]

Eberstadt continued waxing eloquent about the book: "But—don't let this go anywhere but in your library—I cannot urge you more than I have, but I assure you that it is by all odds the best purchase and the most valuable item in the collection—such an item—never again possible to secure—will be worth 10 times the price in association with your other fine material, & will, I assure you, as time goes on, afford you, in its possession, many a happy chuckle, when you compare notes with other collectors—certainly I have had nothing which I would rather see your library have in the past ten years— You will forget the cost—but never the pleasure such a unique item will afford."[66] Happy chuckles or not, Coe passed on the book, and Crocker did buy both the guide and the original manuscript.

One of the quirks of the rare book business is the possibility of a book at auction suddenly surpassing all previous values and selling

---

[63]Charles B. Voorhis to Edward Eberstadt, June 3, 1925. William Reese, Private Collection.

[64]Edward Eberstadt to W. R. Coe, April 8, 1921. Box 8, Eberstadt Records, Beinecke Library.

[65]Dickinson, *Dictionary of American Book Collectors*, 80–81; Henry R. Wagner, "Recollections of Templeton Crocker," *California Historical Society Quarterly* 28 (December 1949), 363–66.

[66]Edward Eberstadt to W. R. Coe, April 8, 1921. Box 8, Eberstadt Records, Beinecke Library.

for a record price. This aspect of the business tempted Eberstadt, and he tried placing material in several rare book auctions in the early 1920s. Eberstadt had a copy of Stephen F. Austin's very rare book on Texas, the *Esposicion al Publico Sobre los Asuntos de Tejas* (Mexico City, 1835). Coe would not have been a customer for a Texas book, since his interest was in the Pacific Northwest. Eberstadt put the book in an auction at Anderson Galleries, along with a large number of other books from the Eberstadt inventory, in 1922.[67]

Eberstadt explained his motivations this way: "Back in the dim and distant days of the early twenties when Huntington, Crocker, Jones and other multis [apparently multimillionaires] of like ilk were dominating the auction room. They just didn't seem to know that poor old Eberstadt existed. In such a situation my devious mind went to work on all four cylinders and came up with the world shaking answer to the problem. All that I had to do to gain a fortune was to quit the book business and go into the auction business."[68]

After this realization, Eberstadt did not waste any time.

I will center my experience upon the above mentioned Austin's *Esposicion*, which appeared in the November 22, 1922 auction sale and brought the astounding price of $1,075.[69] I had estimated that if the Gods were kindly disposed, the piece might fetch $375. What then was my amazement when [rare book dealer] Walter Hill and Dr. Rosenbach proceeded to clash with each other, the one representing Mr. Huntington, and the other Herschel V. Jones, with the result that the huge and hefty price of $1075 was realized. I left the room walking on air. Disdaining to longer ride with the herd in the subway, I hailed a taxi and rode homeward in an air of ecstatic bliss.[70]

The bliss did not last for long. "Came the dawn, and with it a phone call. The Anderson Galleries were on the wire. Mr. Mitchell Kennerly, the entrepreneur of the Galleries, wanted to see me— and pronto. What he told me was that my Austin's *Esposicion* had been returned. The reason therefore being that I had stated in the

[67]*A Great Collection of Original Source Material Relating to the Early West and the Far West* (New York: The Anderson Galleries, 1922).

[68]Edward Eberstadt to James T. Babb, June 14, 1950. Box 35, Manuscripts and Archives, Yale University Library.

[69]*A Great Collection* (1922), lot 32.

[70]Edward Eberstadt to James T. Babb, June 14, 1950. Box 35, Manuscripts and Archives, Yale University Library.

heading to the item that it was 'one of two known copies,' a statement which, it appeared, was entirely too enthusiastic. In fact, not
one more, but several copies had been located. So I took my book
and slunk away from the gaudy halls of fortune."[71] Not all was lost,
however. "But there is an end to all disaster, if not this letter, and so
Brother Kennerly called me sometime later to impart the happy tid-
ings that their client would pay $500 for the item. What would you
do? Okay, me too. I grabbed that V-Note, and thanked God for his
kindly intervention."[72]

Sometimes even a bookseller's mistake—as when an unavailable
copy is inserted in a catalogue at an unbelievable price—can turn
to gold. Eberstadt related a humorous story about his employee and
cataloguer, Seymour Dunbar,[73] to Coe:

> Upon my return from abroad I was greeted with a little catalogue
> which Mr. Dunbar had prepared in my absence and was almost
> floored to find on the last page, catalogued as item no. 299 [in cata-
> logue 82], "The Provisional Laws of Jefferson Territory," which I had
> procured for you and for which I had already sent you my bill for
> $750. I was elated to think that while I was busily striving for books
> in England, Dunbar had turned up right here at home a far rarer item
> than anything I had been able to discover across the sea, but alas this
> was not the case. He needed one more item to complete the catalogue,
> and concluded he would wind up in a blaze of glory, and therefore,
> borrowing my card for your copy of the Jefferson Laws, had this set
> up in print. To make the pyrotechnic display more glorious he affixed
> a price of $3,000 upon the item.[74]

Eberstadt continued with the best part of the story, though: "If seeing the item in print dazed me somewhat, imagine what were my
feelings when the Law Library of Harvard University wrote in and
although somewhat hopeful of a price reduction, asked us to reserve
the item until the return of the head librarian. When I came to I

---

[71]Ibid.

[72]Ibid.

[73]Dunbar was the author of *A History of Travel in America* (New York: Tudor Publishing,
1937) but as a cataloguer had a reputation for occasionally causing problems for Eberstadt;
longtime New York rare book dealer Peter Decker told William Reese that Dunbar was a
"hophead," apparently referring to heroin use.

[74]Edward Eberstadt to W. R. Coe, September 13, 1926. Box 9, Eberstadt Records, Beinecke Library.

wrote the library and told them the item had already been sold, but that should I ever again hear of a copy of the work I would give them first opportunity at it. So far as I have been able to discover, but one other copy of the book exists and I regard it as one of our very choice items."[75]

Eberstadt probably thought this somewhat humorous order from Harvard at the elevated price was the end of the matter, and here is the Harvard librarian's original inquiry that floored him: "Among other items in your catalogue No. 82 we are very much interested in No. 299: Provisional Laws and Joint Resolutions . . . General Assembly of Jefferson Territory. Omaha, 1860. I think, however, that the price asked for the same is much too high."[76]

But somehow another copy of the incredibly rare Jefferson Territory laws turned up during the following year, and Eberstadt sent Harvard a quote, at a reduced price from the "catalogue" price of $3,000. The librarian's response tells the end of the story: "I enclose herewith a check of the Bursar for $2500 in payment of the Laws of Jefferson Territory."[77]

One of the most important aspects of bookselling is determining the price of a rarity. This is especially difficult when an item is unique or unrecorded. Price it too high and it might remain in inventory for a long time; price it too low, and have multiple orders and the regret of missed profits. This is particularly true with manuscript material, where each item is unique.

In the rising market of rare books in the 1920s, even booksellers were sometimes uncertain as to what a certain copy of a rare or unrecorded item should bring. Bookseller Fred Lockley turned up a rare guide, Daniel Lowell's *Map of the Nez Perces and Salmon River Gold Mines* (San Francisco, 1862) and wondered what Eberstadt would offer for it. Eberstadt responded to his inquiry: "You ask me what I will pay for it and in this regard I may state what I have previously written you, that in cases where I have made the price someone else got the books. . . . I can go high as the next man on a given hand of

---

[75]Ibid.

[76]Robert B. Anderson to Hudson Book Company, September 2, 1926. Box 9, Eberstadt Records, Beinecke Library.

[77]Eldon R. James to Edward Eberstadt, December 2, 1927. Box 9, Eberstadt Records, Beinecke Library.

cards, but I am the rottenest long-distance poker player the world ever saw."[78] This was Eberstadt's polite way of declining to be the opening bid for someone else's private auction.

Sometimes even a master book salesman like Eberstadt was thwarted with the challenge of trying to sell a rare book of western Americana that happened to be in a foreign language. Eberstadt had sold Voorhis the important California voyage, Eugène Duflot de Mofras's *Exploration du Territoire de l'Orégon* (Paris, 1844), in French because, as he explained, the original had never been translated into English. Voorhis returned the books with this note: "These I would like to return to you as I am not a Frenchman and never expect to be and I can think of no possible use I could put them to, except to keep for a number of years and then try to find some other sucker who is willing to pay me twice the sum, and I would a lot rather that you make this extra profit than to make it myself."[79]

Eberstadt explained himself thus: "One of the strange things about you which I occasionally forget in trying to view you as a book collector is that you propose to read your books. This is contrary to all the laws of the game, and although I hate to say it, is not entirely fair to me. I have one man who doesn't even open the packages, but he, of course, is an advanced collector."[80] The collector who accumulated the unopened packages of books was Coe, and when Edward's son Lindley came to his Oyster Bay estate to begin the process of transferring and appraising his collection for Yale, he had to begin by opening the packages of books—some of which had sat in an attic for nearly twenty years.[81]

Sometimes, to any rare bookseller's dismay and ulcerating agony, collectors quit. Templeton Crocker, the San Francisco book collector, wrote one of the saddest missives any bookseller can receive from a prized customer. "Now I have been buying a good many books lately, particularly Californiana and I cannot afford to keep on at this rate . . . therefore you had best stop looking around for me

[78]Edward Eberstadt to Fred Lockley, June 9, 1927. Box 9, Eberstadt Records, Beinecke Library.

[79]Charles B. Voorhis to Edward Eberstadt, April 27, 1927. William Reese, Private Collection.

[80]Edward Eberstadt to Charles B. Voorhis, April 30, 1927. William Reese, Private Collection.

[81]Anecdote related by Lindley Eberstadt to William Reese, New Haven, Connecticut.

upon receipt of this letter. . . . I regret that I must cease collecting now for so long a time."[82]

This letter from Crocker—and the loss of his business to the Eberstadts—might have prompted this letter from Eberstadt to Coe just a couple of months later (with every rare bookseller's slight tendency to overexaggeration). Apparently Coe had mentioned giving his collection to the University of Wyoming library someday; in any case, Eberstadt responded: "If you ever give them your collection, every son of Wyoming should take a day off, get down upon his knees and shape a brick, or hew a stone, that goes into the structure which shall house the donation; and I shall want to be there too (though I hope very aged and infirm) and perhaps the spirit will move old Eberstadt to attempt one honest day's work—tragic thought and moment this, and awful in the contemplation—but pshaw! The flesh is weak and the habits of the years will have found me out; tremblingly I'll totter towards the cornerstone of this great monument of your generosity and my crime, and sink me to the earth—it will be the end!" What in most people would be considered overdramatization is from the rare bookseller's perspective merely stating the obvious.

Of course, collectors might quit—but they find it very hard to stay out of the book collecting game. Bishop Thomas had Eberstadt sell some rarities from his western collection to Coe, probably starting sometime in the early 1920s;[83] then he sold the remainder of his book collection with rarities such as John L. Campbell's guidebook, *Idaho: Six Months* (Chicago, 1864) and James J. Strang's *Book of the Law of the Lord* (St. James, Mich., 1851), a Mormon splinter group's book of revelation, and many others to Voorhis in the fall of 1926 for $13,000.[84] Bishop Thomas apparently repurchased most of his collection from Voorhis sometime in 1927, and then in 1929 the remainder of Thomas's western books were sold at auction in New

---

[82]Charles Templeton Crocker to Edward Eberstadt, November 3, 1921. Box 8, Eberstadt Records, Beinecke Library.

[83]See Edward Eberstadt to Charles B. Voorhis, May 12, 1927. William Reese, Private Collection. Some misunderstanding about W. R. Coe's purchase of books from Bishop Thomas exists, largely due to a statement made by Edward Eberstadt in his account of the Coe Collection written for the *Yale Library Gazette*. However, the correspondence clearly shows that Coe purchased books from Thomas through Eberstadt over a number of years.

[84]Charles B. Voorhis to Edward Eberstadt, December 1, 1926. William Reese, Private Collection.

York City in the Anderson Galleries. Perhaps that was when Bishop Thomas decided to retire to Florida, as any sane person who had lived through many Wyoming winters would have done.[85]

Of course, one man's decision to quit collecting can be the beginning of another's lustful desire. Every collector's dream—to buy a library or a collection of rare books in one fell swoop—can also become their biggest nightmare. When Voorhis told Eberstadt that Bishop Thomas was going to sell his library of western books to him, it was probably not without some hesitation on Eberstadt's part, who wondered exactly what the deal would include of the bishop's library—would it include, for example, the collection of western maps?

Eberstadt had wondered what was happening when the bishop asked him to appraise his book collection—was the appraisal for insurance purposes? Or did the bishop want an appraisal for selling his collection? Bishop Thomas was evasive, and Eberstadt agreed to do the appraisal for no charge—after all, the bishop was an old customer who had introduced Eberstadt to a couple of very good customers.

But when the appraisal was finished (coming in at $23,000), Eberstadt heard nothing else about it until Voorhis teasingly told him in September 1926 that he would soon have big news—the big news being the purchase of the bishop's Wyoming book collection for $13,000—some $10,000 less. After the collection was boxed and sent to Voorhis in Wisconsin in November, he told Eberstadt not to ship him any more books for the time being because he was out of space. The initial plan seemed to be for Eberstadt to simply sell the Thomas duplicates for Voorhis: "When Mr. Voorhis returns I shall want to take over the duplicates acquired in the Bishop Thomas collection, and if you have no list of them, let me know and I will make this up and forward to you."[86]

But after they were shipped, Voorhis had no opportunity to get to them for several months; finally, in May 1927 he wrote to Eberstadt in desperation—the dream was becoming a nightmare. "If the Lord will forgive me, I will never again buy a library. . . . I have not yet

[85]Henry R. Wagner to Thomas W. Streeter, October 6, 1938. Box 14, Folder 4, Streeter Papers, American Antiquarian Society.

[86]Edward Eberstadt to Margaret Roberts, undated page. William Reese, Private Collection.

unpacked the boxes which are now reposing in the back room of my office and I am putting off and dreading the undertaking of this checking process and I am just wondering if it would not be better for me to sell this library as is, and trust to my own . . . spiritual advisor in those matters to complete the library which I have started under his direction."[87]

Voorhis's anxiety was palpable. He wondered to Eberstadt if perhaps the collection could not be sold to Phillip Ashton Rollins, who Bishop Thomas said was in the market for Wyoming books, and who did become an important Eberstadt customer. Rollins was an 1889 graduate of Princeton University who had established a successful law practice in New York City and whose family had ranches in the West; according to family lore, when he was five years old (around 1874) he spent time out West under the care of Jim Bridger.[88] Voorhis continued: "In buying the Bishop's library I have bitten off a little more than I can chew. . . . I feel almost helpless in trying to unpack these books and check them over and index them; in fact, I simply haven't the time to do it. Will you not listen to my cry of distress and advise me out of your unlimited experience?"[89]

Eberstadt took a few days to respond, probably weighing carefully the various options before advising his friend and customer. "Regarding the Bishop's library I can well understand the chaos which has resulted from its shipment to you and the dread with which you contemplate unpacking the cases and checking the books."[90]

Eberstadt next reviewed the circumstances leading to the sale of the collection and his role in appraising the collection. "Early last November the Bishop dropped in to see me. We had quite a long chat during the course of which, among other things, he brought up the question of my idea of the value of his collection. I told him that I thought I could appraise it from a checklist, and he told me that he had brought this on to New York. . . . I was entirely familiar with

---

[87]Charles B. Voorhis to Edward Eberstadt, May 4, 1927. William Reese, Private Collection.

[88]See Dickinson, *Dictionary of American Book Collectors*, 270–71; Harold W. Dobbs, "Philip Ashton Rollins, '89," *Princeton University Library Chronicle* 9 (June 1948), 177; Esther Felt Bentley, "A Conversation with Mr. Rollins," *Princeton University Library Chronicle* 9 (June 1948), 178–90; and Thomas W. Streeter, "The Rollins Collection of Western Americana," *Princeton University Library Chronicle* 9 (June 1948), 191–204.

[89]Charles B. Voorhis to Edward Eberstadt, May 4, 1927. William Reese, Private Collection.

[90]Edward Eberstadt to Charles B. Voorhis, May 12, 1927. William Reese, Private Collection.

the library, having gone carefully over it for Mr. Coe some years ago, and purchasing at that time such things as were necessary to the Coe Collection."[91] Eberstadt noted that the appraisal occupied several days of his time, during which the bishop dropped in as well, and "not being utterly stupid I finally reached the conclusion that perhaps you had in view the purchase of the collection."[92]

Next, Eberstadt addressed the question of selling the library to Philip Ashton Rollins, which Thomas had suggested: "Now with regard to Mr. Rollins and the possibility of his purchasing this library. Mr. Rollins is a very heavy buyer, but like yourself he has been acquiring his books through the years and as a consequence has practically everything along his lines which is contained in the Bishop's library. No doubt he would be immensely pleased to purchase the nuggets, but these are the very items which you should keep for yourself."[93] Eberstadt next came to the core of the question; because he had previously selected and purchased the better books for Coe's library, and "what was left I should have regarded as more properly the nucleus for a public library rather than a desirable en bloc purchase for a private collector."[94] Eberstadt recommended culling what was needed for Voorhis's collection, and then donating the remainder to either the University of Wyoming Library or the Wyoming State Library.

In the meantime, Bishop Thomas brought over a few choice nuggets from his collection to Voorhis that had not been packed with the rest, including James J. Strang's *Book of the Law of the Lord* (1856); Thomas J. Dimsdale's *Vigilantes of Montana* (Virginia City, Mont., 1866), John B. Wyeth's *Oregon* (Cambridge, Mass., 1833), Joel Palmer's *Journal of Travels over the Rocky Mountains* (Cincinnati, 1847), a poor copy of James Marsh's *Four Years in the Rockies* (New Castle, Penn., 1884), the amusing *Journey to the Gold Diggins by Jeremiah Saddlebags* (Cincinnati, 1849), and John L. Campbell's *Idaho: Six Months in the Gold Diggings* (New York, 1864) in original wrappers. When writing about this latest part of the acquisition, Voorhis offered to give the Dimsdale to Eberstadt as a "thank-you" gift for his help (since he already had a copy in his collection).[95]

[91]Ibid.
[92]Ibid.
[93]Ibid.
[94]Ibid.
[95]Charles B. Voorhis to Edward Eberstadt, May 14, 1927. William Reese, Private Collection.

Eberstadt responded to the gift offer: "Relative to the Dimsdale, it is extremely generous of you to offer to present this book to me, and while I cannot accept it, I deeply appreciate the sentiment. . . . I sold you your copy for $250 and shall be glad to purchase either copy back for the price paid me."[96] Apparently the bishop had told Voorhis that he thought there was a rich buyer who would pay $750 for a copy of the Dimsdale; Eberstadt informed him, "Relative to the $750 price, I might say that had I been in possession of this book a month or two ago I could have sold it for this figure. At that time Mr. Rollins did not have the book and was extremely anxious to get it to present to Princeton University, but we have since located a copy and that leaves him out of the market."[97] As far as the other rarities, Eberstadt remembered the bishop's Palmer as being in quite poor condition; he offered to take it on and give Voorhis whatever he could sell it for. And since Voorhis did not have a copy of the Wyeth *Oregon* book in his collection, Eberstadt recommended that he keep it. The bishop's copy of the Strang, *Book of the Law of the Lord*, was incomplete; Eberstadt recommended he put that copy in the reject pile, but the Marsh book on Isaac Rose he recommended for keeping as well as the Campbell on the Idaho gold mines: "The Campbell is the finest book yet acquired—in fact, this is a brilliant high light in any collection of Western Americana."[98]

Then, quite unexpectedly, Voorhis received an answer to his supplication: "Much to my surprise, I received a letter from Bishop Thomas today saying that it was his desire to repossess his library, and asking if I would sell it back to him, and if so, to pack it and ship it to Philadelphia. I presume are you familiar with the fact that Bishop Thomas resigned as Bishop of Wyoming, to take effect July 1, and that he is going to Philadelphia as President of the Divinity School there. . . . This seems to be a happy issue out of all our difficulties."[99]

Eberstadt concluded the same as well: "Bishop Thomas' decision to repurchase his collection is the best possible solution of the problem, and I am glad to know that everything has turned out so favorably."[100] Eberstadt concluded that were Voorhis just beginning in

---

[96]Edward Eberstadt to Charles B. Voorhis, June 10, 1927. William Reese, Private Collection.
[97]Ibid.
[98]Ibid.
[99]Ibid.
[100]Edward Eberstadt to Charles B. Voorhis, June 15, 1927. William Reese, Private Collection.

his collecting, the bishop's library would have been a useful acquisition, but that since the bishop was unaware of how many of the desirable items of his library were already owned by Voorhis, this resolved the issue.

The Eberstadt–Voorhis correspondence tapers off after this point, for apparently after giving it some thought over the summer of 1927, Voorhis decided to quit collecting books. Sometime in 1938 he contacted Henry Wagner, stating that he had spent $30,000 on his book collection and wished to sell what was left of them; Wagner told Streeter that he expected Voorhis could only get perhaps half that amount at this point in the Depression.[101] Voorhis later decided to give his collection to Pomona College and in the 1930s donated the land and buildings that became California State University at Pomona.

Some characters in the rare book business, whether dealer or collector, try the patience of those who deal with them. Many antiquarian booksellers will recognize at once what Eberstadt was talking about when he spoke with Coe about the upcoming auction of rare Louisiana books belonging to Robert Schwartz (November 8, 1926): "Schwartz was not at all popular in the trade, and I do not think the sale will be supported. It was Schwartz who, a couple of years ago, demanded that I sell him one of the items which I had set aside for your collection. You may recall the incident. He pulled out a roll of hundred dollar bills enough to choke an elephant, and insisted that his money was as good as anyone else's, but I was obliged to inform the gentleman that he did not possess enough money to buy the item. He then told me that unless he got it he would never buy another book from me, and right there Mr. Schwartz and myself parted company."[102]

Besides a headstrong collector, some of the other most difficult people the Eberstadts had to deal with were "collector-scouts"—someone who collects, but who has to scout and sell other books to finance their collecting. The conflicting interests of such individuals, half-collector and half-bookseller, often land them in tense relationships with the book trade.

---

[101]Henry R. Wagner to Thomas W. Streeter, October 6, 1938. Box 14, Folder 4, Streeter Papers, American Antiquarian Society.

[102]Edward Eberstadt to W. R. Coe, November 5, 1926. Box 8, Eberstadt Records, Beinecke Library. Charles Everitt also has a story about Schwartz asking for a discount in Everitt, *Adventures of a Treasure Hunter*, 79.

The addition of a major collector like Coe in the 1920s increased Eberstadt's need to find more rare books—and to do so he had to deal with some difficult collector-scouts. One of the best known of these was Frederick W. Skiff, who worked as an auditor for Wortman's Department Store in Portland, Oregon (Skiff has even written an autobiography about his collecting adventures).[103]

When Eberstadt visited Skiff in Portland early in 1921, Skiff already knew of a very rare overland narrative, Randall Henry Hewitt's *Notes by the Way: Memoranda of a Journey across the Plains, from Dundee, Ill., to Olympia, W.T., May 7 to November 3, 1862* (Olympia, Washington Terr., 1863).[104] Skiff knew that an early Oregon printer/collector, George H. Hines (who printed the first poems for Joaquin Miller in Oregon in 1871), had a copy of the book on deposit in the Oregon Historical Society library. Hines, who was secretary/treasurer of the society, was reluctant to sell it. While Eberstadt was visiting, Skiff took him to see Hines, who showed them the Hewitt narrative. Later that evening Skiff asked Eberstadt how much that little overland guide would be worth. Eberstadt seems to have taken this after-libation opportunity to pontificate on the value of the book without much regard for the possible consequences, and pronounced it to be worth $500.

After Eberstadt returned to New York, Skiff wrote him in July 1921: "I made Hines an offer for the Hewitt that staggered him."[105] The offer was for $500, and Hines apparently was not the only one who was staggered at the offer. Skiff encouraged Eberstadt to wire the money posthaste. Less than a week later, Skiff was writing to Eberstadt about the Hewitt book again. In his eagerness, and apparently without waiting for Eberstadt to approve the plunge, he purchased the rare pamphlet: "I paid like h— for it and made the offer last week having in mind your figure of 500 . . . it strained the

---

[103]Frederick W. Skiff, *Adventures in Americana: Recollections of Forty Years of Collecting Books, Furniture, China, Guns and Glass* (New York: Metropolitan Press, 1935), which, unfortunately, is one of the most unreadable collecting books I have ever encountered.

[104]This little guide is Wagner-Camp 391, and Howes L457, where it is a "dd"—of the utmost rarity.

[105]Frederick W. Skiff to Edward Eberstadt, July 21, 1921. Box 8, Eberstadt Records, Beinecke Library. The Skiff letters were donated to Yale in 1952 by Edward Eberstadt with the following note: "I have just run into some further letters of Fred Skiff, from whom, as you know, we purchased a considerable body of Oregoniana . . . this is further provenance of the items acquired through him."

exchequer—Can you shoot a check up here instanter?"[106] It seems
evident from this that Hines, as secretary of the Oregon Historical Society, was authorized to sell either duplicate or out-of-scope
materials from the society library, but also that Hines combined
the traits of a raconteur and a horse trader—not bad qualities when
working with scouts and booksellers.

While Eberstadt's reaction is not completely known, it can be
fairly deduced as having placed him in the position of receiving a
fairly severe financial shock (the rough equivalent value of $500 in
1921 to 2016 dollars varies, but it would be fairly close to $10,000). For
a bookseller in Eberstadt's position, it was one thing to remark on
the possible value of a rare book over a dinner conversation, and quite
another to have a scout notify you that they had expended that con-
versational sum on a rare book and needed to be reimbursed, pronto.

Apparently this large outlay—without the prior permission of
Eberstadt—weighed heavily on Skiff's mind. Later that day, using
the telegraphic account of Wortman's Department Store, he cabled
Eberstadt: "Purchased Hewitt narrative today paid for it and have it
in my possession can you conveniently send me a check for five hundred dollars Wednesday Had to pay very high for book Answer."[107]
The next morning his tremendous outlay still weighed heavily on
Skiff's mind, and he wrote Eberstadt again: "I had just deposited
my salary check and could just about cover the item—so my need of
quick return" on the $500.[108]

Just a while later that day, a worried Skiff wrote Eberstadt again:
"I received your letter telling me you don't want the Hewitt—then
your telegram telling me 300 is the top. . . . Hines was dumbfounded at my offer—of course, I never would have bought it except
my thorough belief that you were behind me."[109] Now it was Skiff's
turn to be dumbfounded at Eberstadt's offer of $300.

Eberstadt, with some reflection on the possibilities of future business endeavors with Skiff, seems to initially have declined the book,

---

[106]Frederick W. Skiff to Eberstadt, August 3, 1921. Box 8, Eberstadt Records, Beinecke
Library.
[107]Frederick W. Skiff to Edward Eberstadt, August 3, 1921. Telegram, Box 8, Eberstadt
Records, Beinecke Library.
[108]Frederick W. Skiff to Edward Eberstadt, August 4, 1921. Box 8, Eberstadt Records,
Beinecke Library.
[109]Ibid.

and then to have offered $300—60 percent of Skiff's outlay, but which would still leave him with a substantial deficit. Skiff decided to try to reason with Eberstadt once again and wrote another letter: "Don't get alarmed. . . . When I go after anything I go hard and try to bring home the bacon. . . . You subsequently told me what you would give for it—if I could get it—500 and & I wrote it down."[110]

The next morning an elated Skiff received noticed of a wire for $500 from Eberstadt and telegrammed the following: "Thank you earnestly for your wire this morning—not only does it help me square things financially and close up the worry but it inspires me with full confidence that you are with me so to speak. The Hewitt [is] packed and gone."[111]

While this first venture in rare books ended successfully and the Hewitt landed in Coe's collection, the next foray, when Skiff discovered a trove of original manuscripts dealing with the Whitman massacre in Oregon, would severely test the patience of both parties. Dr. Marcus Whitman led the first overland pioneers to the Oregon Territory in 1847, but his inability to prevent a measles epidemic from killing over two hundred Cayuse Indians led to an attack that killed him and his wife, Narcissa, and eleven other members of his company as well as precipitating the beginning of the Cayuse War.

Just over a month later, Skiff wrote Eberstadt with tantalizing news about an archive of manuscripts about the Whitman massacre: "The historical importance of these letters cannot be overestimated. . . . One folio letter written 5 days after the Whitman massacre telling in detail the events. 48 by Marcus Whitman, dated at his mission . . . these Whitman letters are a complete history of the weekly events of the mission. . . . I don't need to tell you that this lot is almost price-less for I believe you would come out here to secure it. If I land the lot—you shall have first chance at the whole. Will let you know at once."[112]

Less than two weeks later, Skiff telegrammed Eberstadt with his successful news—but this time without plunging on a misunderstood

---

[110]Ibid.

[111]Frederick W. Skiff to Edward Eberstadt, August 5, 1921. Box 8, Eberstadt Records, Beinecke Library.

[112]Frederick W. Skiff to Edward Eberstadt, September 7, 1921. Box 8, Eberstadt Records, Beinecke Library.

price for acquisition. In spite of this, there were still major problems during the negotiations for the collection. "SECURED YESTERDAY ALL MANUSCRIPT ITEMS. . . . GIVING YOU FIRST REFUSAL ON LOT FOR TIME BEING ARE YOU INTERESTED ANSWER."[113]

Eberstadt was probably excited to receive this news, but this time when he answered he exercised some caution and wanted more information—as well as a subtle warning to Skiff not to ask too high a price, no matter how rich Skiff thought his client was. Eberstadt replied that his client was returning to his office this week but that he was feeling the "general market depression," nevertheless, if Skiff bought it at a "satisfactory" price Eberstadt was confident he could place the collection promptly, with the proviso now that Skiff give him the "bedrock spot cash price" for the collection and the warning that Eberstadt had recently "fell down on my Sutter manuscripts account," which was a "bitter lesson."[114]

Eberstadt was perhaps being a bit disingenuous with his warning about the Fort Sutter manuscripts to Skiff, but on the other hand he certainly wanted to secure them at the best possible price, as would any good bookseller. During the previous year, Seymour Dunbar, who worked as a cataloguer for Eberstadt, had prepared a transcript of the thirty-eight volumes or albums of the Fort Sutter manuscripts, which was limited to an edition of twenty copies. The Fort Sutter Archive, which contained the correspondence, orders, and art of Lieutenant Edward Kern from 1846, had been offered to Templeton Crocker in the summer of 1921 at a higher unmentioned price; in August, Eberstadt offered to reduce the price of the collection to the price paid of $6,000, with the exception of the Monterey broadside Proclamation of Independence (which Crocker already had). Crocker passed on the collection, and it was consigned to Anderson Galleries. That worked out successfully; the manuscripts sold in 1921 for $8,450 (and the purchaser was Henry Huntington, in whose library the manuscripts may be seen today).[115]

Skiff was not without his own powers of persuasion when it came

[113]Frederick W. Skiff to Edward Eberstadt, September 21, 1921. Box 8, Eberstadt Records, Beinecke Library.

[114]Edward Eberstadt to Frederick W. Skiff, undated draft of telegram. Box 8, Eberstadt Records, Beinecke Library.

[115]Edward Eberstadt to Chas. Templeton Crocker, August 6, 1921. Box 11, Eberstadt Records, Beinecke Library.

to touting the value of the collection to Eberstadt. He responded to Eberstadt's request for a "spot bottom cash price" and more information on the Whiteman papers with some alacrity, if not acquiescence to the request. The price would be between $3,000 and $3,500 for this almost "priceless collection."[116]

By mid-October, Skiff agreed to accept a $1,500 deposit in return for shipping the Whitman papers on approval to Eberstadt, but over the next two months relations between the two rapidly declined. From Skiff's perspective, he probably wanted to have a quick decision and sale—and payment of $3,250, the eventually settled upon price. For Eberstadt's part, he had already paid nearly half of the asking price and didn't seem to be in hurry. At some point Skiff began sending insulting letters and telegrams to Eberstadt about the situation (unfortunately, Eberstadt did not keep any of the insults).

At any event, in mid-December Skiff wrote to Eberstadt: "I am writing you perhaps for the last time but I am doing so to clear the situation. I am in receipt of a letter which says that you are sore and hurt over my insulting telegrams & letters. . . . Did I do this? Look at the telegram."[117] Skiff was feeling the financial pressure and finally felt compelled to give the details of the bind he was in—he had borrowed a "considerable sum" from his employer, Mr. Wortman, even though Wortman had advised him against the transaction and considered it a "tremendous mistake."[118]

It is not surprising that those with little experience in the rare book trade would be so surprised by large business deals being concluded with handshakes or, more frequently, just a casual conversation (with no follow-up or confirmation emails, either). From Wortman's perspective, Skiff had sent a large and valuable collection across the country without a full deposit for security, and now two months had passed by with no action—no wonder that Skiff, who was probably already prone to worry and anxiety, suffered even more the reminders from his boss about his foolhardy act. And Wortman, too, knowing Skiff's predilection for speculation, was probably worried about how or when Skiff might repay him the borrowed money.

---

[116]Frederick W. Skiff to Edward Eberstadt, September 23, 1921. Box 8, Eberstadt Records, Beinecke Library.

[117]Frederick W. Skiff to Edward Eberstadt, December 15, 1921, Box 8, Eberstadt Records, Beinecke Library.

[118]Ibid.

Eberstadt responded with some pointed reminders of his own (as well as an additional payment of $500 for Skiff) in the following letter: "Some of your remarks were exceedingly discourteous, some more than offensive, and in the case where you went to the extent of questioning the fact of my having made the selection for Mr. Coe, and doubting that there was such a man, as you put it, downright——."[119] Apparently Mr. Wortman had put the question of whether Eberstadt actually had an actual customer for the collection in Skiff's mind, where it gnawed at him.

Eberstadt continued with a slightly more diplomatic approach: "Well there is no use in swapping wicked words, suffice it to say I felt very much chagrined to put it most mildly, and very much hurt. . . . Now with regards to the Mss . . . You must understand that I am dealing with one of the biggest men in this country, this is not a department store executive [a little swipe at Wortman] but a man whose yes or no affects affairs throughout the whole U.S."[120] This was another reminder for Skiff's benefit about who he should be listening to—his boss, or the bookseller who dealt with one of the richest men in the country?

Eberstadt appealed to Skiff's more worldly side: "Here we have the chance of a life-time Skiff. . . . I have before now talked myself hoarse telling you the possibilities; and I can only hope that your calmer judgment will show you which is the wiser course."[121] Eberstadt was finally able to conclude the deal with Skiff, and the collection was sold to Coe.

There is one postscript to this story that sheds some light on Eberstadt's efforts to acquire original materials relating to the Whitmans. Clifford Drury, a Presbyterian pastor and independent historian (author of the two-volume *Marcus and Narcissa Whitman and the Opening of Old Oregon*) had found eight original letters from the Whitmans while on a scouting trip in Idaho, and he decided to stop by Eberstadt's on a visit to New York.

Drury noted that Eberstadt paid him little attention when he introduced himself as a visitor from Idaho who wished to see his

---

[119]Edward Eberstadt to Frederick W. Skiff, December 21, 1921, Box 8, Eberstadt Records, Beinecke Library.

[120]Ibid.

[121]Ibid.

stock of western books. Eberstadt's interest in the visitor rapidly changed when Drury "informed him that I had eight old original Spalding letters with me—down came his feet, he spun around and asked to see them. I showed them to him, and he at once asked me to set a price. He was eager to buy them. 'No,' I replied, 'these are already sold to the Presbyterian Historical Society.'"[122] For any bookseller, this is the ultimate tease—a great group of manuscripts of historical importance, but not for sale. Eberstadt, though, had not played this game for many years for nothing. Drury said that Eberstadt tried every possible means to get him to part with the letters, when he told Drury, "'Reach out and touch that safe,' he said pointing to a large safe near my chair. 'In it,' he added, 'is a collection of sixty Whitman letters.'"[123]

Drury found himself the pleader: "'Let me see them,' I begged. 'No, the bloom would then be off the peach,' he said. So I never got to see those letters before my first Whitman biography appeared in 1937."[124] True enough, but probably the letters already belonged to Coe and were not Eberstadt's to make decisions about. Ultimately, Drury was able to use the letters in his biography after they were deposited at Yale.

Eberstadt's extroverted personality was most unusual among the generally introverted world of book collectors and rare book dealers. He cultivated lifelong friendships that endured even through the natural competitions and rivalries that embellish the collecting game. Good-natured and not-so-good-natured competition between dealers and collectors is part of the rare book game. Eberstadt once went to Salt Lake City to buy the original manuscript journal of William Clayton—author of the most useful and famous overland guidebook, *The Latter-day Saints' Emigrants Guide* (St. Louis, 1848)—from the Clayton family.

Dr. Widtsoe, who had been president of the University of Utah had just resigned to become Secretary to the President of the Mormon

---

[122]The Presbyterian Historical Society had already agreed to reimburse Drury for the $50 he had paid a descendant for the letters; during his lifetime Drury continued the altruistic practice of locating institutions for all archival materials he found.

[123]Clifford M. Drury, "Reminiscences of a Historian," *Western Historical Quarterly* 5 (April 1974), 143.

[124]Ibid.

Church.[125] On my arrival he asked me to come over to the Church Office and have lunch with him. He then exploded the bomb under me. "Eberstadt," said the mighty dignitary, "you got Egan's journal out of the state, but you are just one day too late on the Clayton records; they became the property of the Church yesterday afternoon. So be it. The Church and I are good friends but we have had some interesting tussles and I expect I will have others since I cannot concede they have a divine right to such historically valuable material as may be discovered within the bounds of their jurisdiction."[126]

At any rate, the victor was in a magnanimous mood since Widtsoe invited Eberstadt on a two-week journey that summer through Bryce Canyon in southern Utah.

Eberstadt had a close relationship with two of his key customers, Philip Ashton Rollins and Thomas W. Streeter. Rollins typed an imaginary overland account sometime in 1929 for the amusement of his dealing and collecting friends, Eberstadt and Streeter, "Across the Plains in the Days of the Most Costly Overland Narratives."[127] In the "narrative," Rollins, Eberstadt, and Streeter set out with this entry, "Grass continues scarce. Forgot to mention we are bound for California. Will we ever reach there? No one knows. Passed a grave today. Its occupant bid $70 at an auction, got a Western book worth more than said sum, and they buried him where he dropped."[128]

After passing the grave of the startled collector, the three bookmen continued when "Doc. Braislin [William C. Braislin was a doctor and alum of Princeton who sold his western books at auction in 1927][129] announced he'd sold out his collection and was going back to the States. Streeter and I keep on with Eberstadt. Eberstadt says that now, being west of the Missouri River, he understands

[125]John A. Widtsoe was later a member of the Quorum of the Twelve Apostles of the Church of Jesus Christ of Latter-day Saints (LDS).

[126]Edward Eberstadt to Charles B. Voorhis, May 26, 1925. William Reese, Private Collection. The LDS Church Historical Library also has letters from Edward Eberstadt to John A. Widtsoe dated January 20, 1923; February 6, 1923; February 26, 1923; March 7, 1923; March 13, 1923; March 29, 1923; and April 1, 1923, all relating to the purchase of duplicates from the LDS Historical Library.

[127]Since published as a keepsake with a preface by William Reese; Philip Ashton Rollins, *Across the Plains in the Days of the Most Costly Overland Narratives (with Map of the Trail)* (New Haven & Princeton: Overland Press, 1978): 400 copies printed at the Stinehour Press for the Overland Press; the original at Yale came in the papers of Charles Eberstadt.

[128]Rollins, *Across the Plains*, 11.

[129]Dickinson, *Dictionary of American Book Collectors*, 48.

the local signboards and knows them to be reliable. They all read 'E. E. $37.50,' though some old-timers say they used to read 'E. E. $15, Scarce.'"[130]

Rollins had his share of fun with this jab at Eberstadt's prices, along with a poke or two at Streeter's proclivity for vast collecting: "Passed Chimney Rock, which is a great natural curiosity. Guide book says it is not as big as it used to be. Found reason why. All that has disappeared is in Streeter's collection."[131] Rollins concluded with these sage words for those who might embark on a collecting trip with a dealer like Eberstadt: "Stock up your wagons with nothing but cash, for the dealers resent your wasting any money on food."[132]

Good-natured ribbing between dealer and collector seemed often to be a part of rare book collecting with Eberstadt. On New Year's Day in 1926, Eberstadt received the following telegram from his collector, Voorhis: "Dear Booklegger, May the New Year bring much joy and contentment to you and your family and notwithstanding the illegal nature of your business I trust you escape the enforcement officers."[133] Eberstadt could not resist approving of such a title: "A Booklegger! The term is a masterstroke."[134]

Eberstadt was not only developing his rare book business in the 1920s but also his passion for western history scholarship and publishing ventures. Walter Prescott Webb, the great western scholar, once wrote to Eberstadt asking him why his publications were done in limited editions. Eberstadt responded, "Of course, it is unfortunate, as you say, that books of this character are published in so few copies, but one has to be guided by the present demand. Were the book a new novel by Harold Bell Wright, perhaps an issue of a million copies would be too few, but old Doctor Experience warns me to print as few books as possible on any worth-while topic."[135]

---

[130]Rollins, *Across the Plains in the Days*, 12. Doctor Braislin sold his western Americana collection at the Anderson Galleries in 1927.

[131]Rollins, *Across the Plains*, 13.

[132]Rollins, *Across the Plains*, 15.

[133]Charles B. Voorhis to Edward Eberstadt, December 29, 1925. William Reese, Private Collection.

[134]Edward Eberstadt to Charles B. Voorhis, January 6, 1926. William Reese, Private Collection.

[135]Edward Eberstadt to Walter Prescott Webb, December 2, 1926. Letter tipped into a copy of Lorenzo Sawyer, *Way Sketches* (New York: Edward Eberstadt, 1926), belonging to Michael D. Heaston, Wichita, Kansas.

Among the books Eberstadt edited and published were original sources of western travel and adventure, including the very ambitious and rare thirty-nine-volume set edited by Seymour Dunbar and with a preface by Edward Eberstadt [which was limited to twenty copies], *Transcript of the Fort Sutter Papers* (Edward Eberstadt, 1921); Joseph Williams, *Narrative of a Tour from the State of Indiana to the Oregon Territory in 1841–42* (Edward Eberstadt, 1921); *John Colter, Discoverer of Yellowstone Park* (Edward Eberstadt, 1926); Lorenzo Sawyer, *Way Sketches: Containing Incidents of Travel across the Plains from St. Joseph to California in 1850* (Edward Eberstadt, 1926); and a two-volume set edited by Seymour Dunbar, the *Journals and Letters of Major John Owens, Pioneer of the Northwest Coast* (Edward Eberstadt, 1927). All these publications today are considered valuable contributions to historical research, and many still command premiums in the antiquarian book market.

By the end of the 1920s Eberstadt, with his strong customer base and his growing reputation, was a powerful figure in the world of rare book collecting. However, this expensive and rarified world was vulnerable to economic pressures, and the stock market crash of October 1929 was disastrous. In the coming Depression, Edward Eberstadt would not only find his finances and book business affairs strained to the limit, but he also faced the challenge of bringing his two sons, Lindley and Charles, into the family business. As always, Eberstadt's passion and creativity rose to the occasion.

2

Selling Books
in the Great Depression
1929 ❧ 1940

In the early 1930s, one visitor recorded his impressions of Edward
Eberstadt after a visit. "His office was high up in a Forty-
second Street building overlooking the New York Public
Library. I found him leaning back in a swivel chair, his feet on the
windowsill, enjoying a glass of liquid refreshment."[1] Edward's office,
northwest of the library at 55 West 42nd Street, would have offered a
fine view of the New York Public Library's gardens, though his win-
dow contemplations in the 1930s were probably more often about the
changing national economic climate and the depressed state of the
rare book trade.[2]

Eberstadt had a penchant for speculating in the stock market,
perhaps influenced by watching some of his more successful customers, such as Coe and Streeter. Like many others, he had enjoyed
speculating in stocks as prices rose in the late 1920s, but the crash on
October 24, 1929, suddenly meant margin calls for cash that strained
his emotions and business.

As the stock market crash became the Great Depression, several schemes to raise money were thought of—at one point, even

---

[1]Drury, "Reminiscences of a Historian," 143.
[2]On the depressed state of the book trade in the early 1930s, see Charles F. Heartman's
editorials in *The American Book Collector* 1 (January 1932), 3–4; 1 (April 1932), 199–202; 1 (June
1932), 329–32.

Streeter, who was squeezed for cash, suggested that Eberstadt take some of Streeter's rarest overlands to California to show and try to sell to Estelle Doheny (who used her oil fortune to collect California and the West, among other passions).[3] But when Streeter asked his friend Henry Wagner what he thought of that plan, Wagner discouraged it, saying that Doheny was not actively purchasing.

When the Doheny idea did not pan out for Streeter, he spoke to Eberstadt about selling some of his rarer books to Coe: "About two weeks ago I worked out with Eberstadt a tentative scheme to sell a few of my rarest overlands to Coe, who has been very much interested in getting them, and has talked to Eberstadt from time to time about them."[4] In addition, Streeter also sold some of his rarest American colonial books to Lathrop Harper, who never tried to sell them but waited until his friend and customer could afford to buy them back.

Even a major financier like Coe was affected by the Depression, and this may have played into his decision to resell some of the materials back to Streeter. Streeter related to Wagner that "Eberstadt saw Coe last Friday about some Western material which was coming up at a sale, and found him in a very depressed state of mind, not wanting to buy anything—writing a letter to his plantation in South Carolina discharging most of the help, and so on—so that temporarily, at least, there is nothing from that source."[5] Years later, after Streeter had improved his financial situation, he was able to have Eberstadt repurchase some of the rarer materials for him from Coe.

Wagner responded to Streeter with some sage words about rich people in depressing times: "Coe acts just like lots of other rich people, getting sick before they are very much hurt. That is a well-known phenomenon in periods of depression. Nobody kicks as hard as the man who has lost half of $100,000 income, except possibly the man who has lost half of a $1,000,000 one."[6]

At this time (some months after the 1929 crash) Edward wrote to Everett Graff after sending him a copy of the rare overland by Overton

---

[3] Dickinson, *Dictionary of American Book Collectors*, 94–95; Ellen Schaffer, "Reminiscences of a California Collector: Mrs. Edward Doheny, 1875–1958," *Book Collector* 14 (Spring 1965), 49–59.

[4] Thomas W. Streeter to Henry R. Wagner, May 31, 1932. Box 14, Streeter Papers, American Antiquarian Society.

[5] Ibid.

[6] Henry R. Wagner to Thomas W. Streeter, June 2, 1932. Box 14, Streeter Papers, American Antiquarian Society.

Johnson and William H. Winter, *Route across the Rocky Mountains* (Lafayette, Ind., 1846): "I am billing at $625 on account of the damn stock market and its cruel pranks on my bank roll. Two months ago I sold the copy I bought from Mr. Mitten for $750—and maybe, if I keep guessing at the other fellow's game a while longer—I will be selling gold double-eagles for $10. Please stay *at work* Mr. Graff, I need a few clients who don't get this easy money we hear about."[7]

When the oilman Everette DeGolyer ordered some books from Catalogue 94 in the spring of 1930, Eberstadt responded: "Its publication [Catalogue 94] is a silent testimony to my at least temporary divorce from Wall Street and now if you will only do as well for me in the oil situation as you have consistently done in connection with books, all will be well, for I have held on to my oil stocks, and if these ever come back, I will be able to once again put on my spats and strut forth with my cane, as in the boom days of 1929."[8]

As Edward mentioned, he did not give up investing in those oil stocks, and the mood of speculation must have seized him mightily. In a later letter he added a handwritten note about the oil company of which DeGolyer was president, and in which Eberstadt had gone short (betting that the stock price would continue to decline): "*WHY* didn't you tell me Amerada was going to hop upwards? Do you want me to keep starving?"[9]

As the economy occasionally showed signs of recovering in the 1930s, Eberstadt continued his speculation in the stock market, including complaining good-naturedly to Graff, the president of a steel company: "What the hell is the matter with Bethlehem Steel Preferred? I thought I was very smart when I dropped out with a ten point profit in the 70s. However my cupidity got the best of me and I essayed another whirl in it. I have now accumulated four lots at entirely new and hitherto unplumbed bottom[s]. My last acquisition was at 42. Today I see they are trying to find buyers for the damn stuff at 36. Oh, mister, what is a poor girl going to do?"[10]

---

[7]Edward Eberstadt to Everett D. Graff, no month or day, [1930]. Box 4, Folder 3, Graff Papers, Newberry Library.

[8]Edward Eberstadt to Everette L. DeGolyer, April 16, 1930. DeGolyer Library, Southern Methodist University.

[9]Edward Eberstadt to Everette L. DeGolyer, June 5, 1930. DeGolyer Library.

[10]Edward Eberstadt to Everett D. Graff, May 2, 1932. Box 4, Folder 2, Graff Papers, Newberry Library.

Despite this lament, it seemed difficult for Eberstadt to stay out of the market. Later he wrote to Graff on stock speculation: "My short position in U.S. Steel is still maintained, but the darn stock is strong as all hell."[11] Graff responded that that sentiment alarmed him since, as a steel executive, he speculated that the prospects for U.S. Steel would continue to be strong. "I was rather shocked that you were still short, and I don't want your blood to be on my hands."[12]

Streeter was concerned about Eberstadt's penchant for investing and the effect on his health, as he related to Wagner: "Until a few days ago, I had seen practically nothing of Eberstadt for the last three months. He has been rather morose and under the weather. I had a nice visit with him about a month ago, and he called me on the phone this morning, quite upset over the failure of the Harriman Bank, here in New York, to open, as he and his wife are both depositors there."[13]

Later, during another stock market correction in the fall of 1937, Edward wrote to DeGolyer, now in Texas: "Do you remember way back in '29 when the old stock market went fluey and ruin and disaster stared us all in the face?"[14] Eberstadt related that a hefty order from DeGolyer saved him on that "calamitous day": "I need not tell you that I shall never forget it."[15] Eberstadt then confessed that he still liked to speculate in the stock market, but the correction in October of 1937 (an average loss of 49 percent) had caught him extremely out of pocket. Edward expressed his thanks again to DeGolyer for the most recent and timely order:

> Mr. DeGolyer, your letter came at just another of those psychological moments when all hell—and a particularly personal hell—broke loose and began to singe and burn me like nobody's business. When some months ago I sent you that telegraphic S.O.S. I had been riding the market short for damned near a year. Them 750 bucks of yours enabled me to keep my position for almost another week. Then I was forced

[11]Edward Eberstadt to Everett D. Graff, April 3, 1936. Box 4, Folder 1, Graff Papers, Newberry Library.

[12]Everett D. Graff to Edward Eberstadt, April 6, 1936. Box 4, Folder 1, Graff Papers, Newberry Library.

[13]Thomas W. Streeter to Henry R. Wagner, March 13, 1933. Box 14, Folder 2, Thomas W. Streeter Papers, American Antiquarian Society.

[14]Edward Eberstadt to Everette L. DeGolyer, October 28, 1937. DeGolyer Library.

[15]Ibid.

out and the God damned market started down. A case in point was Westinghouse Electric. I went short just above par and was finally forced to cover at 158. Our mutual friend, Tom Streeter, was so darned worried that when I covered I wrote him telling him I was out of it.[16]

Edward concluded, "The whole game's a great see-saw and of course a fellow's a damned fool to ever get down. Nevertheless, as I say, your letter brought me all the way back to 1929. It was a pat on the shoulder and seemed to say, 'Buck up—what the hell's the difference anyway?'"[17] This aspect of Edward's personality—his penchant for investing and speculating in stocks—was probably not too far removed from the character traits that led him into rare books—an area much more successful for him.

In the midst of the Depression, Lindley and Charles Eberstadt joined their father in the rare book business immediately after graduation from college. This may have been in part because of the national economic depression and in part due to Edward's declining health, undermined by his proclivity for alcoholic refreshment. Sometime in 1931 Lindley (a graduate of Columbia University) began working in the business, writing to a customer that "Dad is once again laid up, this time with a touch of the Grippe."[18] Edward's other son, Charles (a graduate of Brown University), was working in the rare book business by 1933, and in 1935 the business name became Edward Eberstadt & Sons, with Lindley's name (as oldest son) in the upper-left corner and Charles's in the upper right of the letterhead. Interestingly, the first catalogue with Edward Eberstadt & Sons was number 111 (1938).

As Lindley and Charles came into their father's rare book business, they each brought different strengths that would contribute to the success of the firm. Lindley was by nature very personable; he developed close relationships with many collectors and became the traveling book scout and salesman for the business. Charles, who was quiet and scholarly, brought his research skills to cataloguing and describing the rare books. He was primarily responsible for the acclaimed catalogues the firm issued over the next three decades, though he carried on cordial and friendly relations with collectors as

---

[16]Ibid.
[17]Ibid.
[18]Lindley Eberstadt to Everette L. DeGolyer, November 9, 1931. DeGolyer Library.

well. It is remarkable that both brothers were passionate about their father's business and able, not only to continue it, but to help it prosper for the next thirty years. Although more common in Europe, few American antiquarian book firms have been carried over to the second generation—making the Eberstadts even more remarkable.

One early letter illustrates the research skills Charles used in the preparation of the Eberstadt catalogues and the delight he took in finding bibliographic points—minor variations in typesetting or format used to distinguish editions and printings—that were items of concern to collectors. He wrote to Beulah Rollins, wife of collector Philip Ashton Rollins, who also took an active interest in bibliographical points of western Americana: "I think I have discovered a point on Joel Palmer's *Journal* which may interest you. From Wagner's note the only way to ascertain the first issue is to note whether the preliminary leaves are not present. However the second issue was actually reset and the word 'grassy plains' is changed from 'sandy plains' on line seventh from the bottom, p. 31. Also on page 121, line fourth from the bottom the first issue reads 'the company own from six to eight mills above the fort,' which is corrected as 'the mills are six and eight miles above the fort.'"[19]

One of the most important aspects of cataloguing is the contributions to bibliography it affords, and one of the landmark bibliographies for western Americana is the guide to overland narratives published between 1800 and 1865 compiled by Henry R. Wagner, *The Plains and the Rockies* (San Francisco, 1921). Wagner privately printed this bibliography in 1921 in an edition of 250 copies, and the edition sold out almost immediately. Edward once wrote to historian Walter Prescott Webb explaining the importance of this work: "Wagner spent many years in the compilation of this bibliography which deals, as its title indicates, with all printed narratives of an original nature in relation to the trip across the plains. It is certainly

---

[19]Charles Eberstadt to Beulah Rollins, February 16, 1939. Philip Ashton Rollins Collection, Department of Rare Books and Special Collections, Princeton University Library. Streeter wrote of Beulah: "Mrs. Rollins was tremendously interested in building up the collection and personally supervised the research incident to compiling its catalogue. She knew the books and their authors well and little escaped her keen eye." Thomas W. Streeter, "The Rollins Collection of Western Americana," *Princeton University Library Chronicle* 9 (June 1948), 203. Some enterprising rare book librarian should write an article documenting Beulah's contributions to the Rollins Rare Book collection at Princeton.

the most valuable bibliography of the West which has ever been prepared. Some years ago, when in California, I purchased the last remaining three copies from Mr. Wagner, and I have one copy left which I will quote to you at $35.00. I do not care to part with it, however, and unless you feel that the book is necessary to your work and that you must have it, I very much prefer to keep it myself."[20]

The 1921 edition of the Wagner bibliography remained the most important reference work for western Americana until the publication of the second edition in 1937. This edition was the first edited by Dr. Charles L. Camp, a paleontologist who had met Wagner in an antiquarian bookstore while Camp was still a graduate student at Columbia University. Camp later became director of the Museum of Paleontology at the University of California at Berkeley but never lost his enthusiasm for California and western history.[21]

Edward had apparently promised to send any new information along to Camp for the 1937 edition before it was published. When this information was not forthcoming, Wagner wrote: "I wrote to Eberstadt a couple of weeks ago and hauled him over the coals for not sending the information about the *Plains and the Rockies* that he promised, but if he is as sick as you think there is not much likelihood that I am going to get an answer or receive the information. . . . I would also like to get from Eberstadt some indication as to whether Coe has anything that I do not know about or not."[22]

After the publication of the bibliography, Edward noted that many of the detailed points about issues were used by Camp without attribution to him. He wrote to Beulah Rollins, "I spent last night going over the Wagner-Camp bibliography. One or two things irritated me somewhat. For instance, I noted in the 'Editor's Note' that our mutual friend Mr. Graff had taken the unwarranted liberty of sending on to Dr. Camp the private notes which I had made in my copy of the former edition. I feel that this was a violation of

---

[20]Edward Eberstadt to Walter Prescott Webb, December 2, 1926. Letter tipped into a copy of the Lorenzo Sawyer, *Way Sketches* (New York: Edward Eberstadt, 1926), belonging to Michael D. Heaston, Wichita, Kansas.

[21]Anonymous, "Charles L. Camp (1893–1975): Third Director of the University of California Museum of Paleontology," University of California Museum of Paleontology, www.ucmp.berkeley.edu/about/history/clcamp.php (accessed April 20, 2015).

[22]Henry R. Wagner to Thomas W. Streeter, April 23, 1935. Box 14, Folder 2, Streeter Papers, American Antiquarian Society.

a confidence."[23] This is understandable; trade secrets, which can include special points of collation or information about editions, are a rare bookseller's most valuable tools—and to have them published without permission for the world to see evidently upset Edward.

The question of Camp borrowing his notes without attribution stuck in Edward's craw for a bit longer; in February of the next year he wrote Beulah Rollins: "I don't know whether you saw Mr. Ticknor after the tea at the Grolier Club the other evening. . . . We had about a half hour's talk and I gave him a list of the various errors which I had found in the new edition of *The Plains and the Rockies*. How many of these he will use I know not, but if he goes into the matter at any length the article should be of considerable interest. Of course he knows nothing of the subject I am telling you! He does know his Louisiana however, and also he swings a mean pen. Hip, Hip, Hooray!"[24] Apparently Edward was hoping for a bit of vindication and retribution to Wagner via a poor review of his bibliography.

One of the weaknesses of Wagner's overland bibliography is the cut-off date of 1865.[25] This meant that any account of the trip made before 1865 but published afterward would not be included in the bibliography. Eberstadt had noticed this weakness and approached the Chicago collector Everett Graff with his idea of expanding the bibliography:

> The more I have gone into the thing, the more I am convinced of the essential need of a similar tool wherein the overland narratives of contemporary origin, but of later printing, would find due record. Basically, it seems to me, the student and the collector as well, is interested not so much in the question of *when* a book was printed as in what the book tells about. Certainly there is room for this second volume, and equally certain is it would create both an increased interest and a very reasonable augmentation in the value of the books so listed. We have spoken of this on several occasions. What do you think of it? And if

---

[23]Edward Eberstadt to Beulah Rollins, September 1, 1937. Rollins Collection, Princeton University Library.

[24]Edward Eberstadt to Beulah Rollins, February 2, 1938. Rollins Collection, Princeton University Library.

[25]I can only speculate that Wagner choose this date as an ending for his bibliography since it was the end of the Civil War, but a much more appropriate closing date for the overland bibliography would have been 1869, the year that the transcontinental railroad was completed.

a favorable view is entertained would you consider collaborating with me in the preparing and editing of such a volume?[26]

Apparently Graff agreed to the proposal of a joint collaboration, because later Edward reminded Graff, "Now Everett, don't forget that you agreed to join with me in preparing a bibliography of the narratives printed from 1865 onward. Charles has been putting in considerable time on this, and is slowly bringing the bibliography into shape. Sometime next summer, if convenient to you, he would like to make a trip to Chicago and spend some time with you in checking up and collating your collection of this subject."[27]

While Graff may have been too busy with his business concerns to work on this project, he did write to Charles to encourage him in the bibliography project as soon as he returned from the war: "I still feel the truth of what I told your father many years ago—that any complete bibliography of overlands published since 1865 would cover a great deal of ground. I do sincerely hope that you will take hold of this job again and complete it and I will be delighted to help you to the extent of books in my library and my notes when you get around to where you need them."[28] Charles did compile a typed list in 1938 that was circulated in a few copies, but the project apparently never went beyond this point.[29]

Collaborations of this sort, successful or not, are indicative of the close relationships the Eberstadts forged with their customers and colleagues. The other tradition that Lindley and Charles continued after joining their father was assisting in the publication of the firm's scholarly works and original sources of history, including James Bennett, *Overland Journey to California* (Edward Eberstadt, 1932); Robert Stuart, *Discovery of the Oregon Trail* (Edward Eberstadt &

[26]Edward Eberstadt to Everett D. Graff, July 2, 1935. Box 4, Folder 2, Graff Papers, Newberry Library.

[27]Edward Eberstadt to Everett D. Graff, March 18, 1936. Box 4, Folder 1, Graff Papers, Newberry Library.

[28]Everett D. Graff to Charles Eberstadt, October 17, 1945. Box 3, Folder 15, Graff Papers, Newberry Library.

[29]Charles F. Eberstadt, *An Abbreviated Title Preliminary Check List in Preparation for a Bibliography of "Modern" Narratives of the Plains and Rockies* (1938), 29 pages (543 entries). Interestingly, this project has been continued by a California collector, Mark Mortenson, with a typed list entitled *Crossing the Plains: Overland Narratives Printed after 1865 Including the Eberstadt Modern Overland List* (which now comprises some 1,401 entries).

Sons, 1935); and a rare Indian captivity narrative, Emeline L. Fuller, *Left by the Indians: Story of My Life* (Edward Eberstadt, 1936).

Even though the two brothers were working full-time in the firm, Edward continued to contribute his goodwill and salesmanship to the operation. It seems clear the Edward enjoyed holding court with interested potential collectors, and it probably did not take much interest on the part of the collector to draw him out. Earl Vandale, an oil-leasing agent for the Magnolia Oil Company who built a very important collection of Texana, first visited the Eberstadt store in November 1934, and the next day Edward wrote him, "How time flew yesterday! When I got home—I carry no watch—I was amazed to learn it was nearly midnight. How can you forgive me for chattering at such unconscionable length. Biography is interesting; autobiography more so; but monologues! Ye Gods. I am reminded of the man who was self-made and thoroughly in love with his creator."[30] This self-deprecating chatter was typical of Edward's humor.

But Vandale remembered the evening spent in the bookstore with pleasure: "I want to reprove you for referring lightly to the afternoon and evening we spent together. To me it was a most wonderful experience, and I was deeply, profoundly and intensely interested." As any book collector knows, it can be a lonely passion and difficult to interest others in the latest hunt and newest acquisition. Vandale admitted, "I was so engrossed, and the time sped so swiftly, that it startled me when I arrived at the hotel and saw the lateness of the hour. It really embarrassed me, and does yet, to think I detained you so long." Vandale concluded, "The day is likely an incident to you but to me it is a treasure remembered vividly."[31]

However, in the highly competitive world of rare book collecting, egos and personalities could easily clash and cause personal and professional problems. Edward once had to soothe the ruffled feathers of a dealer who apparently had an unpleasant encounter with Everett Graff. Lindley had purchased a rare book from the Kansas City antiquarian bookseller, H. N. Sender, who had sold him a copy of the rare John E. Cox, *Five Years in the U.S. Army* (Owensville,

---

[30]Edward Eberstadt to Earl Vandale, November 16, 1934. Earl Vandale Papers, J. Evetts Haley Collection, Nita Stewart Haley Memorial Library, Midland, Texas.

[31]Earl Vandale to Edward Eberstadt, November 24, 1934. Vandale Papers, Nita Stewart Haley Memorial Library.

Ind., 1892) on one of his trips west. Sender had strictly instructed Lindley that the book was not to be offered to Graff, but somehow Sender learned that shortly afterward Graff had purchased a copy of the book from the Eberstadts and indicated his displeasure.

Edward wrote to Sender to calm the upset bookseller and to explain how their firm had acquired a second copy of this book: "I suppose next to the top divas in the Metropolitan Opera House there just ain't anybody on earth so temperamental as a real, sure, honest to God old bookseller. . . . One moment we are up in the air and thinking that all the world and everybody in it is just too perfectly wonderful, and then all of a sudden we veer in another direction and are perfectly certain that all the world and his wife is our bitterest enemy, and out to get our scalp."[32]

Collectors and bibliographers, of course, could be just as difficult and headstrong as dealers. Eberstadt wrote to Beulah Rollins to see if she had heard anything about the feud between Merle Johnson, a noted bibliographer of American literature, and Charles F. Heartman, an antiquarian bookseller and auctioneer known for his strong personal opinions.[33] Heartman had published a review of Merle Johnson's *Checklists of American First Editions* in his magazine, *American Book Collector* (December 1932) that began, "Before me lies a new edition of this book. I wish by heaven I could say something good about this book."[34] Edward continued, "It appears in the last issue of the Collector and is about as tart a castigation—if a castigation can be tart—as I have read in a month of Sundays. I have been expecting almost any day to pick up the paper and read of a duel out Metuchen way [Heartman's hometown in New Jersey]."[35]

Sometimes friendly perseverance goes farther with antiquarian booksellers than almost any other strategy. Edward had been trying to acquire a rare collection of letters from the Colorado Pike's Peak

---

[32]Edward Eberstadt to H. N. Sender, May 19, 1936. Box 4, Folder 1, Graff Papers, Newberry Library.

[33]Edward Eberstadt to Beulah Rollins, January 3, 1933. Rollins Collection, Princeton University Library.

[34]Charles F. Heartman, "The New First Edition Check List," *American Book Collector* 1 (December 1932): 367. A biography of Heartman's many contributions and personality would make an excellent addition to the literature of the rare book world.

[35]Edward Eberstadt to Beulah Rollins, January 3, 1933. Rollins Collection, Princeton University Library.

gold rush from William Todd, a rare book dealer in New Haven, Connecticut. Apparently another bookseller had tried to preempt the Pike's Peak letters, and Todd vented that it was because of "the low caste Jews that are in it and the bum lot of book scouts that are cutting each other's and everyone else's throats."[36] Unfortunately, this anti-Semitic attitude was quite common among both collectors and dealers at this time. Todd finally decided to reduce the price of the collection after all these problems and told the patient Eberstadt: "Our relationship has been so long and pleasant and the owners of the letters were so anxious to get money, that I let it go."[37]

There are few things in the rare book trade that bring out the natural competitiveness like an auction. There is also some strategic thinking about competitors that goes into auction planning as well. Sometimes a dealer will discover something crucial about a lot that, hopefully, remains unknown to others—known in the trade as a "sleeper"—unless someone else "wakes up" and finds it as well.

Edward wrote to Coe about a preview at an upcoming auction that had such a sleeper:

> And now to a matter of more importance. You will remember that when I last saw you I mentioned the discovery of a copy of the Stuart Overland Journal; this item was originally offered by Mr. Harzof [Max Harzof, a New York rare book dealer][38] but when I came up from Florida to see him about it, he told me that the lady who left it with him on consignment had decided to put it up at public auction, and had accordingly taken it from him and placed it with the American Anderson Galleries. From what he told me of the manuscript, I inferred it was not a contemporary copy, and did not feel very especially enthused about its purchase.[39]

Eberstadt went to the auction preview of the journal with the western collector Philip Ashton Rollins, but when they examined

---

[36]William Todd to Edward Eberstadt, undated, no box number, Curatorial Files of Western Americana, Beinecke Library, Yale University. The animosity against Jews appears more than once in the collectors' letters I have read (though never in the Eberstadts' correspondence).

[37]William Todd to Edward Eberstadt, undated, no box number, Curatorial Files, Beinecke Library.

[38]Dickinson, *Dictionary of American Antiquarian Bookdealers*, 94.

[39]Edward Eberstadt to W. R. Coe, April 30, 1930. Box 8, Eberstadt Records, Beinecke Library.

the manuscript it required only the merest glance to perceive that it too was actually written by Stuart.

> Of course, we both tried to give the impression that such was not the case, and that the item had very little importance or value, in view of the fact that the original journal itself, keep by Stuart while crossing the plains, was in existence, and that what was offered was merely a copy, which as I stated to Mr. Smith, was very probably made many years afterwards. However, it now seems evident, and in this Mr. Rollins agrees with me—that because of the difficulty in reading the original, [Robert] Stuart upon his arrival in New York, sat himself down and rewrote the journal for submission to Mr. Astor, and what the auction house is offering is this contemporary copy.[40]

Edward continued describing his auction strategy to Mr. Coe. "Mr. Rollins is belittling the book among his book-buying acquaintances and I of course have done the same so I have hopes we may be able to procure it for a small sum, but should this not be the case my advice is to go after it hard. . . . And now just one final word. If you drop into the galleries to look at the volume (and please do so), do not display any enthusiasm, although I know I am 'carrying coals to Newcastle' to presume to give you advice in such a matter."[41] Apparently Eberstadt's strategy was successful and they obtained the journal.

Sometimes Edward found himself in the very uncomfortable position of having to choose which collector to offer a book to. As long as neither collector finds out, all is well, but occasionally a bookseller comes into a publicly offered book that is hotly desired by two collectors. In this case, Graff and Streeter both wanted a book that Eberstadt had purchased first from the catalogue of the New Haven dealer William Todd.

Graff had visited with Eberstadt in early February and wrote him shortly after the visit, "I was so impressed by your anxiety to get the item from Todd that I would surely like to see it, so if you get it please send it along."[42] Eberstadt wrote sometime later why he was unable to show Graff the rare pamphlet:

---

[40]Ibid.
[41]Ibid.
[42]Everett D. Graff to Edward Eberstadt, February 10, 1936. Box 4, Folder 1, Graff Papers, Newberry Library.

Relative to the little booklet from Todd which as you may recollect was listed by him at $7.50 and which as I wired him I had previously sold for $60.00; I got it. But alas, our mutual friend Tom Streeter also got the Todd Catalogue and he not only telephoned to Todd but also telegraphed to him for the item. In addition to which, around midnight he telephoned me from Morristown and requested—figuratively on bended knee—that in the event I was successful in acquiring the book that I send it pronto to him. Well, Everett what could I do? You knew of the book before Tom did but you did not ask me for it. . . . In this case the fault is yours and not mine. Had you said to me that evening that you wanted the book I could not have done otherwise than tell Tom you had given me an order for it, but as the situation was there was nothing else for me to do than to make delivery to him. As you know, I try to play no favorites. I think you also realize that I deliberately put aside items in which I think you may be interested and withhold them from other eyes. My idea is that each of my friends should have first chance on at least some of the things which I may luckily turn up. It is a hell of a situation at the best, but I try to be fair.[43]

There was no easy resolution for Edward, who was caught between two of his good friends and customers, but his tact and honesty went far in preserving the relationships with each collector.

This is just one example of keen competition between collectors. Once Graff was having lunch with another collector, Donald McKay Frost, a lawyer from Boston who collected western Americana,[44] and the Chicago bookseller Wright Howes.[45] Howes mentioned in passing that he had a telegram from the Eberstadts asking for his newest catalogue, which they had heard about from Streeter. Graff told Eberstadt that Howes's newest catalogue was still at the printers, and even that he had not seen the proof sheets yet.

Graff continued:

---

[43]Edward Eberstadt to Everett D. Graff, February 20, 1936. Box 4, Folder 1, Graff Papers, Newberry Library.

[44]See Dickinson, *Dictionary of American Book Collectors*, 126–27. Frost's collection of western Americana went to the American Antiquarian Society; see "Donald McKay Frost," *Proceedings of the American Antiquarian Society* 68 (April 1958), 8–11.

[45]For more on Wright Howes, see John Blew, *The Lives and Work of Wright and Zoe Howes and the Story of U.S.iana* (Chicago: Privately printed, 2014); Dickinson, *Dictionary of American Antiquarian Bookdealers*, 102–103; William Reese, "Pioneering in Western Americana," *AB Bookman's Weekly* (October 8, 1984), 2336; Jeff Dykes, "Wright Howes," *AB Bookman's Weekly* (October 8, 1984), 2372–73.

I have always been interested to learn Streeter's method of operating and have been trying for years to learn how he always gets the desirable items on every list. But never until now have I had confirmation of the fact that he knew the contents of dealers' catalogues before the proof sheets were out. It must be an expensive thing to maintain an organization of operatives in the printing establishments throughout the country. . . . Just the other day I wired Dawson [a Los Angeles rare book dealer] for several items on an interesting list, figuring that I got the catalogue a day earlier than you and Streeter, but Lo! and Behold! I found all the good items gone and the report was that T. W. S. had them.[46]

Whenever large amounts of money come into a collecting area, there will occasionally be the forgery of rare items (even though uncommon) to warn clients about. Edward's sons continued the same warm relationship with the firm's closest clients, which included warnings about forgeries. When concerns arose about a forged overland narrative, it was Lindley who wrote to Beulah Rollins to warn her not to purchase a fake that they had just uncovered: "This is just to put you on your guard, though we know you would not be fooled anyhow, against a fraudulent overlander that has just turned up. One client of ours purchased it before we heard about the item and we want to make sure that no one else is victimized." The book, purported to be by Joseph Taylor, was entitled *A Journal of the Route from Ft. Smith, Arkansas to California in the Year 1849, with a Full Account of the Trail . . .* (Bowling Green, Mo., 1850). Lindley added, "It is a fairly cleverly done thing. However, on looking into it more thoroughly there is no question whatever concerning its invalidity."[47]

Sometimes desperate booksellers will offer another dealer's rare book in their catalogue without asking permission first. There are obviously a number of reasons why booksellers don't like this, one being that it can make a rare book look more common in the antiquarian market. Streeter reported a case like this to Wagner:

---

[46]Everett D. Graff to Edward Eberstadt, February 9, 1943. Box 3, Folder 15, Graff Papers, Newberry Library.

[47]Lindley Eberstadt to Beulah Rollins, November 18, 1939. Rollins Collection, Princeton University Library. There is a file in box 28 of the Edward Eberstadt & Sons Records, Beinecke Library, Yale University, labeled "Overland Fakes," but it seems to relate to faked typed overland narratives by J. McEwee and J. B. Shaw, both of whom traveled from Illinois to California; there is a typed sheet in the folder, apparently done by Charles, showing a comparison of the similarity of the two diaries.

"Eberstadt is all stirred up over [Arthur H.] Clark[48] advertising the Abbey narrative [James Abbey, *A Trip across the Plains*, New Albany, Ind., 1850][49] for $200 as Eberstadt says that Clark doesn't have it and I guess he is right. Eberstadt says Clark tried to get the copy Eberstadt sold me, which is in wrappers but he never saw it and described it as bound. Eberstadt drafted a vitriolic letter to Clark which he showed me and I told him to forget it and not give Clark the satisfaction of knowing that he has got his goat."[50]

Lindley Eberstadt also learned about shrewd purchasing of library duplicates from his father. When Wagner heard about Lindley's visit to the Bancroft Library in 1936 (where he traded some manuscripts for duplicate printed materials), he vented to Streeter. Of course, Wagner was a book collector without much interest in manuscripts, and so did not think much of this trade: "Lindley Eberstadt made a big haul at the Bancroft Library where he got about $1500 worth of duplicates [printed materials] for about $75 worth of documents, much to the disgust of everybody in the library except Dr. Bolton [Herbert Bolton, the noted historian who particularly sought manuscript sources on the Southwest]. I suppose you will have some of these offered to you. . . . The best thing he got was J. H. Carson's *Early Recollections of the Mines* (Stockton, Ca., 1852). It is not only important but excessively rare."[51]

Streeter was later able to report to Wagner that his hunch about the rarities from the Bancroft was correct. Among the haul from Lindley's California trip that Streeter purchased from the Eberstadts was the Carson book, which Streeter noted was included in Philip Hanna's *Libros Californios* as one of the "twenty rarest and most important books dealing with California," along with several other rarities including Brigham Young's *Second Epistle . . .* (Salt Lake City, 1849).[52]

---

[48]Arthur H. Clark Sr. was an antiquarian bookseller and publisher of western Americana in Glendale, California. See Dickinson, *Dictionary of American Antiquarian Bookdealers*, 33–34; Robert A. Clark and Patrick J. Brunet, *The Arthur H. Clark Company: A Bibliography and History, 1902–1992* (Spokane, Wash.: Arthur H. Clark, 1993).

[49]Interestingly, Midland Rare Book Company had a copy of this book in 1945 for $600.

[50]Thomas W. Streeter to Henry R. Wagner, June 7, 1938. Box 14, Folder 4, Streeter Papers, American Antiquarian Society.

[51]Henry R. Wagner to Thomas W. Streeter, April 13, 1936. Box 14, Folder 3, Streeter Papers, American Antiquarian Society.

[52]Thomas W. Streeter to Henry R. Wagner, April 14, 1936. Box 14, Folder 3, Streeter Papers, American Antiquarian Society.

In spite of Edward's considerable experience, even he occasionally missed a highly desirable and underpriced book in a catalogue. But at least when it happened to him, Edward could find some humor in the situation. An Alabama dealer, J. R. Gardner Jr. of Birmingham, sent out a one-page mimeograph list entitled "Lowest Priced Book List That You Ever Received in Your Life." A priced list with that title would be more than enough to stir the cockles of any bookseller's heart. Buried near the bottom of the first page was this gem: "*Emigrants Guide to the Gold Fields of Idaho and Nevada.* Chicago 1865. Very rare and priced very cheap. $12.50." Apparently this was the second edition of John L. Campbell, *Idaho and Montana Gold Regions* (Chicago, 1865), though listed with an erroneous title.

Eberstadt missed ordering the book but wrote to Graff to find out who had purchased it: "I had quite a shock the other day on opening an envelope from Alabama and seeing a list of trash quoted by one J. R. Gardner. Sticking out in this list like a sore thumb, however, was the 'Emigrant's Guide.'"[53] Edward noted that this was the second time he had missed purchasing this rare book (the previous copy had been advertised for five dollars). Graff was successful in finding out that Chicago antiquarian bookseller Morris Briggs was the successful buyer of the Montana gold guide but wrote that he passed on the book because it was lacking the rear wrappers and at least two pages of text.[54]

Edward had hoped to purchase the guidebook for Philip Ashton Rollins, whose western book collection eventually went to Princeton. He told Beulah Rollins, who was active in her husband's collecting endeavors, the disappointing news: "You may recall my asking if you had heard of the Campbell's Idaho and Montana Guide which was offered in a catalogue from Alabama issued some 10 or 12 days ago at $12.50. This is to let you know that I was unsuccessful in securing it, my telegram arriving just after the dealer had sent it to Mr. Briggs of Chicago." (Morris H. Briggs was a rare book dealer in Chicago from the 1920s to the 1950s.)[55]

---

[53]Edward Eberstadt to Everett D. Graff, January 4, 1932. Box 4, Folder 2, Graff Papers, Newberry Library.

[54]Everett D. Graff to Edward Eberstadt, January 6, 1933. Box 4, Folder 2, Edward D. Graff Papers, Newberry Library, Chicago. Briggs also authored *Buying and Selling Rare Books* (New York: R. R. Bowker, 1927) at the height of the first-edition collecting boom.

[55]Edward Eberstadt to Beulah Rollins, January 6, 1933. Rollins Collection, Princeton University Library.

Edward continued: "Upon hearing this I airmailed Mr. Briggs and he advises me that the price of the pamphlet is $300. This of course is very tragic. The effrontery of anybody asking me to take my own medicine! Mr. Briggs hasn't borrowed a leaf from my book but seems to have purloined the entire volume." Eberstadt might have considered purchasing the volume except that it was imperfect (lacking two leaves).[56] Edward then advised Beulah Rollins that he would not purchase the Montana guide for her unless she particularly wanted it.

Everette DeGolyer once wrote Edward about his own find of a rare overland in a box of books belonging to his partner in the oil business, which took place "right under my very nose."[57] DeGolyer knew that Eberstadt loved a good book discovery story and continued: "My partner, L. W. MacNaughton, who is a lover of books but no collector, has told me a number of times of having a group of old books which were given to him twelve or fifteen years ago by the widow of a geologist friend of his who recently died, and has suggested that I ought to look at the books."[58]

Such boxes rarely have anything of value, and the expert must find a way to gently let down the owner's expectations. DeGolyer continued: "I have promised to do so many times but procrastinated until three or four days ago when he brought a dozen volumes down to the office, most of them were late editions and uninteresting. The one among the lot which was really of interest was a copy of Johnson and Winters' *Route across the Rocky Mountains* (Lafayette, Indiana, 1846)."[59]

DeGolyer continued: "I took the copy home and compared it with my own copy purchased from you and found that the difference was that the MacNaughton copy was bound in black cloth, apparently a contemporary binding. I told MacNaughton the book was valuable and he called me up that night to tell me he had still another copy. The second copy was bound in green boards with a cloth back strip, the same as my copy."[60] DeGolyer had paid the Eberstadts $500 for his copy back in 1929 (before the stock market crash); what would the Eberstadts offer him for these two copies?

[56]Ibid.
[57]Everette L. DeGolyer to Edward Eberstadt, December 26, 1939. DeGolyer Library.
[58]Ibid.
[59]Ibid.
[60]Ibid.

Edward wrote back: "I note too the very telling point you make when you refer to those dear old days back in '29 when you paid us $500 for not two but one copy of the Johnson. God, but what a lot of water has run under the dam since then, eh? Damn damn."[61] Apparently Eberstadt offered $250 in trade for each of the Johnson and Winters guides that DeGolyer had found. DeGolyer wrote quickly back that the book was still valuable: "I do not know at what price you hold your Johnsons, but when I was in Chicago last month Wright Howes priced one at $500."[62] Ultimately Edward acceded to the desire of his client, DeGolyer, instructing him to send the two copies on at "any arrangement for them which will please you, will be entirely satisfactory to us."[63]

In fact, dealers find their books far more prosaically, from other dealers, and more occasionally collectors, book scouts, and auction houses. One exciting story of a previously unknown overland narrative prompted Edward to write to his good collector, Everette DeGolyer, in 1931:

> Last year Morris Briggs of Chicago sent out a catalogue which came to my office on the day I was driving up to Providence to see my kid's team get trounced by Yale.[64] Just as we set out on the drive I felt what the ladies call a premonition; it came to me that I ought to drop by the office before hieing Brown-wards. Mama agreed—her intuition coming to the fore—so down I came.[65]
>
> Well in the Briggs list, item no. 1, plastered across the page in large caps was the thrill of a life-time—the offering of an unknown overland—the Riley Root narrative! It was the biggest kick I've had in years. I decided a telegram would be hopeless; so I grabbed the phone, asked for Chicago, and prayed! God listened in, for in a few minutes Briggs helloed. Mastering my trembling throat muscles and attempting to speak calmly, I inquired, in what I tried to make a casual manner, if the Root narrative was on hand. . . . Yes, it was. . . . Well, well, well!! Being safe, I breathed and proceeded to query the price (it was $950.00). Could he make it somewhat more attractive? No—he could not—it was the best thing ever discovered, etc. etc.[66]

---

[61]Edward Eberstadt to Everette L. DeGolyer, April 25, 1940. DeGolyer Library.

[62]Everette L. DeGolyer to Edward Eberstadt, May 4, 1940. DeGolyer Library.

[63]Charles Eberstadt to Everette L. DeGolyer, May 13, 1940. DeGolyer Library.

[64]Lindley Eberstadt was the elder son and a 1932 graduate of Columbia University; see *New York Times* (June 1, 1932), 16; Charles graduated from Brown University.

[65]Edward Eberstadt to Everette L. DeGolyer, November 18, 1931. DeGolyer Library.

[66]Ibid.

Eberstadt continued with the story of his triumph: "Two days later the booklet came, with the bill and a letter which began: 'Dear Eberstadt: You sure beat the gun on the Root Narrative. Just after you got off the wire Mr. Rollins phoned for it, and I have since been busy telling people all over the country the book is sold—among them, the Ayer Library of this city [Chicago] and the Huntington Library in California.'"[67]

Henry Wagner heard about the rare guide being offered, and his curiosity was piqued. He wrote to Briggs, who told him that Eberstadt had bought the Riley Root narrative. Wagner wrote to Edward asking if he would prepare an article about the narrative for the *California Historical Quarterly*.[68] Eberstadt took eight months before submitting the article, not because it wasn't written, but "I have held up sending it until now as I did not want the title to become known until I had exhausted all possible means of tracing the Root family, and if a copy still remained of the book, of trying to pry it loose."[69]

Edward's perseverance in the search for rare treasures was admirable, even if not always initially successful. Edward told DeGolyer he had been working on finding any additional copies for the prior eight months.

It seemed hopeless as Briggs spent a couple of hundred dollars advertising in the Galesburg papers [where the Root narrative was printed]; had the town searched and gave up at last without having found a trace of the book or family. Some months ago I located Root's granddaughter—a venerable old lady—in Michigan. Yes, she recalled the book, and knew of some other members of the family that had once had a copy, etc—etc—etc. *Patience.* Two months later she wired she had finally gotten the book. Did she send it on to me? No siree. She sent it to a friend in New York for a valuation. His estimate was somewhat flexible. It was worth about $800, possibly a $1,000, maybe even $10,000—I'm serious, that was the report I got back, but with it the tidings that she had found one other copy in the family and several in 'grandfather's old trunk,' (which proved strictly true) although the mice had chewed the lower portion of them away.[70]

[67]Ibid.

[68]Edward Eberstadt, "The Journal of Riley Root," *California Historical Quarterly* 10, no. 4 (December 1931), 396–405.

[69]Edward Eberstadt to Everette L. DeGolyer, November 18, 1931. DeGolyer Library.

[70]Ibid.

After this report, Edward took little time in deciding what to do, and "grabbed the first time table" for a train trip. "We had a heart to heart talk and I finally purchased her 'immensely valuable' library, including the Root Narrative."[71] Eberstadt, tongue in cheek, then listed the other "gems" of the library he had had to purchase in order to secure the copies of the Root narrative (including several religious tomes and textbooks). "I hope you get the same thrill out of this book that I did. Mr. Streeter was incoherent; just gasped, took me to dinner, & finally blurted out, 'Great God, Eberstadt—that's wonderful.'"[72] Everette DeGolyer's own invoice for the book, $600, on November 17, 1931, has the following handwritten notes added by Edward:

> WARNING!!
> [Skull & Bones]
> PREPARE FOR A THRILL!
> *Be Calm Oh Heart—Do not Break*
> *Deep in Love—But Cannot Spake*

The wonderful ending for the three collectors—DeGolyer, Streeter, and Rollins—was that each got his own copy "without wishing to murder the guy who got the copy I got from Briggs."[73] That guy, of course, was Eberstadt's most important customer, Coe. Since then, it seems apparent that Eberstadt wound up with several more copies as well in that haul, since each copy that has turned up in the market since then has also been uncut and untrimmed—a sure sign of remainder volumes.[74]

Occasionally a rare book treasure is found much closer to home—in your own storeroom, for example. Sometime in 1939 Edward apparently asked his sons to clean out the storeroom, but in the process, someone (perhaps Charles) found a great Edgar Allan Poe rarity bound in a volume of pamphlets.

The little rare book was the first printing of Poe's *The Murders in the Rue Morgue*, and the only previous copy found ten years earlier had sold to a collector for $25,000. The *New York Times* reported that Charles and Lindley Eberstadt had decided to "clear out a

---

[71]Ibid.
[72]Ibid.
[73]Ibid.
[74]William Reese is the source of the information on the Riley Root.

storeroom in which old books and pamphlets and an assortment of material had come from many sources." In the process, Poe's work was found in a bound volume of pamphlets, and Charles apparently compared it with the copy in the Morgan Library. As to the value, the Eberstadts told the *Times* that because of the depression it was probably only worth about $15,000—and also perhaps because it lacked the wrappers.

In any event, it made its appearance in catalogue 114 in 1939 (number 667).[75] It did not sell, but that did not keep the Eberstadts from adding facsimile wrappers and offering it in 1947 for $20,000 (catalogue 123). But even the Eberstadts had to acknowledge that it was difficult to sell outside of their own specialty, and the Poe made its final appearance in catalogue 134 in 1954, at the reduced price of $5,000. Facsimile wrappers were much more of an issue (and price difference) for literature collectors than for Americana collectors.

Librarians, who might sell or trade duplicates from their collections, are one occasional source of rare books. In the summer of 1938, a librarian at the Denver Public Library asked the Eberstadts about purchasing a couple of rare books by Alfred Mathews (*Gems of Rocky Mountain Scenery* and *Pencil Sketches of Colorado*), apparently on behalf of a library patron. Edward wrote back, "Ever since your two Mathews books came to hand I have been striving might and main to make up my mind one way or the other about them."[76]

It is important to remember that this was still several years into the Great Depression. Edward continued by stating that he had just bought a beautiful copy at a reasonable figure, and he still had two other copies on hand. "So you see I am rather well stocked, and I do not feel that under the circumstances—and considering the condition of the books—that I can go quite so high as your client wishes."[77] The order department replied on October 5 that the client would accept $125 for both books, and the Eberstadts, still in no great hurry to expend the funds with other copies on hand, finally accepted the offer on October 26.[78]

[75]"Rare Poe Edition Is Unearthed Here," *New York Times*, April 1, 1939, 21.

[76]Edward Eberstadt to John VanMale, September 1, 1938. Edward Eberstadt & Sons Records, Western History & Genealogy, Denver Public Library.

[77]Ibid.

[78]Charles Eberstadt to John VanMale, October 26, 1938. Edward Eberstadt & Sons Records, Denver Public Library.

Edward was good at teasing interest in customers about potential books for their collections. Streeter reported to Wagner that "Eberstadt is back from Europe now, but I have not seen him yet as he went west immediately. I got a characteristic note from him this morning (written from the West) in which he says, 'Think of the half-dozen books you'd most like to have and then rest easy—if you can—in the knowledge that I have at least two of them.'"[79] Streeter later reported, "The book that I wrote you about a while ago and which Eberstadt described in his characteristic fashion was [Thomas] James' *Three Years among the Indians and Mexicans* [Waterloo, Ill., 1846]. I think this is a fine book, and I am delighted to get it even though I had to pay $2500 for it. Another book I got from Eberstadt at the same time is [John L.] Campbell's *Idaho* [1864] the Chicago edition with the appendix about Montana. This book is not in Coe's collection, and Eberstadt says he never saw it before."[80] Both books were fine prizes for any collector; the James is an especially rare narrative of the western fur trade, and the Campbell book contains early information on the Montana (then known briefly as Idaho) gold rush in 1864.

Streeter continued with news of his acquisitions to Wagner: "I haven't seen Eberstadt for a long time, but I am on his trail, and expect to see him within the next few days. He has been away a great deal this summer. While he was away, his office got a very nice copy of the Ingalls narrative [Eleazer Ingalls, *Journal of a Trip to California across the Plains in 1850–51*, Waukegan, Ill., 1852], in nice printed wrappers which he sent over to me. He wants $575 for it, which I should think is pretty reasonable. As you say in your bibliography you never saw it, and as far as I know there are only two other copies—one owned by Coe, the other by Rollins. If I buy it, I will have to keep it a dark secret from my wife. In fact, I am worrying how I can manage to smuggle into the house the Texas books I bought."[81]

A collector missing a book is always a sad creature, even more so when it is a good buy and just missed. Streeter had seen a copy of one of the rarest overland guidebooks, Langford Hastings, *Emigrant's*

---

[79]Thomas W. Streeter to Henry R. Wagner, September 11, 1929. Box 14, Streeter Papers, American Antiquarian Society.

[80]Thomas W. Streeter to Henry R. Wagner, September 24, 1929. Box 14, Streeter Papers. American Antiquarian Society.

[81]Thomas W. Streeter to Henry R. Wagner, September 8, 1932. Box 14, Folder 1, Streeter Papers, American Antiquarian Society.

Guide to Oregon and California (Cincinnati, 1845), in a catalogue of the Smith Book Company.[82] The guidebook was catalogued at $300, but unfortunately Streeter had to run to a director's meeting of his bank. Later that afternoon, "I called up Eberstadt to see if I shouldn't buy it. He was very keen about it—said the price was cheap—and urged me to telephone for it. I did and found out that about an hour before it had been shipped on approval to Graff, of Chicago, who of course will keep it."[83] Wagner commiserated with him: "I am sorry to hear that you missed getting the Hastings Guide. You know I never owned a copy of it, always much to my regret. After I had sold my books to Mr. Huntington, Eberstadt turned up a copy with original wrappers and as he probably knew I was not very much interested he only asked $400 for it, but that was just $400 too much at the time."[84]

In early 1938 Streeter was one of the directors of the Prudence Bond Company. The board had asked him to be president of the company, but he was reluctant because he really wished to retire from outside business and devote his time to such projects as his Texas bibliography. Finally, though, he took the job and wrote to Wagner: "I told Eberstadt I am really working for him now as I took the job to be more certain to have money to spend on books than for any other reason."[85]

The economic recovery by the end of the decade, and Streeter's increased income, meant that he could contemplate purchasing books he had passed on previously. For example, the copy of Mathews's *Pencil Sketches of Colorado* (about which Edward had remarked the high price to Coe) was still unsold by Adolph, of the Cadmus Book Shop at this time, and Streeter thought about buying it for his collection: "I took a little off this noon and went up to see Stager in his new shop at 18 West 56th Street. He had a Mathews *View of Colorado* which he wanted $400 for. He has had it for a good many years. I don't think I am enough out of the woods yet

---

[82]Probably Bertram L. Smith, of Cincinnati, Ohio, who operated a five-story antiquarian bookstore named Acres of Books in the 1930s; see Dickinson, *Dictionary of American Antiquarian Bookdealers*, 203–204.

[83]Thomas W. Streeter to Henry R. Wagner, October 10, 1935. Box 14, Folder 2, Streeter Papers, American Antiquarian Society.

[84]Henry R. Wagner to Thomas W. Streeter, October 17, 1935. Box 14, Folder 2, Streeter Papers, American Antiquarian Society.

[85]Thomas W. Streeter to Henry R. Wagner, March 14, 1938. Box 14, Folder 4, Streeter Papers, American Antiquarian Society.

financially to buy it," he wrote Wagner.[86] Streeter added a post-script: "Just called up Eberstadt to tell him I was writing you. He wanted to be remembered and said he was going to write you in a few days. He says the Matthews is not worth anything like $400—he has a copy which he will sell much less."[87]

Streeter had not given up on getting some of his books back from Coe either. "I had lunch with Eberstadt a week ago today and had a nice time as usual. He is spending a lot of time down at William R. Coe's place on Oyster Bay in unpacking boxes of books that Coe has been buying for the last twenty years. Most of them are still in the original packages from Eberstadt. Eberstadt says there are quite a number of Texas pieces he bought for Coe because they went cheap and which Coe is willing to let me have for a reasonable price."[88] This is not too surprising, since Texas did not fall within Coe's main area of collecting interest.

Unfortunately for Streeter, Coe did not really care to sell anything, though he was open to trading, as Streeter reported:

Also, Eberstadt has finally worked out a trade between Coe and me under which I give Coe a copy of Zamarano's Aviso [a very important piece of California printing] and Coe gives me various Texas pieces he bought at auction in the 1920s when I was hard up and was not buying anything. One of the pieces was the pamphlet printed in Mexico City in 1822 giving the documents about the grant in Texas asked for by Sam Houston and others. There are a couple of broadsides printed in Texas, all around 1836, and possibly two or three other pieces. Ed only closed the deal with Coe the day before Christmas and he is going down there in the next week or so to get the pieces.[89]

Both collectors were satisfied with the deal worked out by Edward.

Streeter later found another rarity from Eberstadt, which he told Wagner about:

I have seen Eberstadt from time to time and have had a couple of nice talks with [Lathrop] Harper, who sailed for Europe last week. I

[86]Thomas W. Streeter to Henry R. Wagner, June 27, 1933. Box 14, Folder 2, Streeter Papers, American Antiquarian Society.

[87]Ibid.

[88]Thomas W. Streeter to Henry R. Wagner, July 22, 1938. Box 14, Folder 4, Streeter Papers, American Antiquarian Society.

[89]Thomas W. Streeter to Henry R. Wagner, December 27, 1938. Box 14, Folder 4, Streeter Papers, American Antiquarian Society.

got from Eberstadt the other day the most interesting little pamphlet about Chorpenning which must have been printed about 1860 and which told about the interferences with his mail by Indian attacks which were specified one by one. The most interesting feature of all was a large map giving the mail routes and indicating where the different Indian attacks took place. Eberstadt told me that years ago he got from someone in Pennsylvania a collection of about fifteen Chorpenning pamphlets but that he had never seen this one before.[90]

Sometimes collectors would write asking about a new interest of theirs. Everette DeGolyer wrote that he wished to add something about the New Mexico outlaw Billy the Kid to his collection; Edward responded: "Dear God, How did you know that Billy the Kid and I were pals?"[91] Edward continued by telling him about a rare wanted poster for the Kid, which was issued by Sheriff Jim Dalton of Santa Fe, around 1880 or 1881 (this same notice appeared as an advertisement in the Santa Fe newspaper and was in Coe's collection). Then, with a typical Eberstadtian flourish, he signed himself—appropriately for one who considered a good customer like DeGolyer as something close to deity—"Pope Edward I."[92]

Every collector has books that they dream of finding someday; these are not "rare" books like a first edition of Lewis and Clark or the *Book of Mormon*, which, while expensive are not necessarily rare. The truly rare are those books that are almost never seen for sale. Into this latter category falls a memoir of the Texas outlaws, the Marlow brothers. (The John Wayne movie *The Sons of Katie Elder* was loosely based on their story.) The Marlows had been wrongly jailed in Graham, Texas, on charges of stealing horses. Local citizens threatened a lynch mob, and one night a crowd of forty or so men tried to get them to leave the jail, but the quarters were so small the Marlows were able to fight off the mob even though they were only armed with a lead pipe. Within a day or two of this attack, the sheriff decided to move them from Graham to another jail in a presumably safer town. He shackled the four brothers to each other in two pairs, but that night when they were being transferred, a large lynch mob attacked the wagon.

---

[90]Thomas W. Streeter to Henry R. Wagner, August 11, 1939. Box 14, Folder 4, Streeter Papers, American Antiquarian Society.
[91]Edward Eberstadt to Everette L. DeGolyer, undated but circa 1945. DeGolyer Library.
[92]Ibid.

Two of the brothers were killed, but the other two, even though each was shackled to a dead brother, were able to fight off the mob. Eventually the charges were dropped, and the two surviving Marlow brothers were able to sue and collect $6,500 for the death of their three brothers (the third was poisoned and then shot shortly after the melee). Later, the brothers moved to Ouray, Colorado, and began ranching. They also wrote a small memoir, *Life of the Marlows As Told by Themselves* (Ouray, Colo., 1892).[93] Earl Vandale, the determined Texas collector and Eberstadt customer, had heard of this book when he visited Graham, and his desire for a copy of the book took a high place on his collecting priorities.

Vandale was told by an old-timer who had read the book as a boy that his father, living at Graham, still had a copy. But some enterprising person had burned all the old man's junk and the book was not found. Vandale set out for Graham and found that many had read the book but no one there had a copy. Then business took him to Denver and the rare book store of Fred Rosenstock, who only had a fragment of the book, and "after much soul searching Fred let him have the fragment for $37.50, disclosing he had traded H. M. Sender, the Kansas City dealer, out of this tantalizing tidbit."[94] But Vandale's next trip to Kansas and visit to Sender yielded only a lead in Marlow, Oklahoma, where an old lady had turned up the fragment that was sold to Sender. Vandale was unable to find anyone who had a copy.

It is not difficult to imagine the thrill Vandale must have felt when he opened the following letter from Lindley Eberstadt in 1943 about the Marlow book: "Yes, we recently discovered another and better copy of this interesting item, though the wrappers seem to differ somewhat from your description, and instead of salmon colored, they are yellow. For your information, I am enclosing herewith a detailed collation. We got $150 for the other copy, but in this case, I will make a price of $125 to you."[95] Lindley took the opportunity in that pre-photocopier era to make a hand-sketch of the cover wrapper

---

[93]There was also a 1927 reprint done in a different binding but with no indication that it is a reprint; sometimes booksellers think they have the rare 1892 edition when they actually have the reprint.

[94]J. Evetts Haley, *Earl Vandale on the Trail of Texas Books* (Canyon, Tex.: Palo Duro Press, 1965), 27–29.

[95]Lindley Eberstadt to Earl Vandale, February 9, 1943. Earl Vandale Papers, Nita Stewart Haley Memorial Library.

of the copy that went to Vandale; it had five oval portraits of the brothers, with their first names on a small scroll below each portrait.

Sometimes even library directors, such as Clarence Brigham at the American Antiquarian Society, picked up rare books on their own from which they hoped to profit. After Dr. Brigham visited with Charles in New York, Charles wrote: "I mentioned last night to Dad your Mexican incunable which you said you wanted to convert into cash to something more in your particular interests. I was somewhat hazy as to the exact title, except that it was a Molina vocabulary."[96]

Brigham responded:

> The 16th century Mexican imprint which I own is [Alonso de] Molina's *Vocabulario en Lengua Mexicana y Castellana*, 2 vols. (Mexico City, 1571). It is in excellent condition except for a scarcely recognizable repair on one of the title pages. I still think that the book is worth from $100 to $150, and I should want at least $90 for my copy. My memory may be wrong, but I think that not a perfect copy of this book has been sold at auction in this country in the last thirty years. I bought this copy in England and think I paid 20 pounds for it. But since that time I have rather lost my interest in early Mexican printing, and furthermore, folio books do not fit any too well into my private library.[97]

While no copy of the Molina appears in the Eberstadt catalogues at this time, it does shortly show up in Wright Howes's catalogues between 1937 and 1940, and that may be where Brigham's copy landed.

In spite of the joshing and occasional competition between bookseller and collector, Edward and Philip Rollins shared a close relationship. They cooperated on the publication of Robert Stuart's Montana journal (the manuscript of the journal was owned by Coe), and at one point Eberstadt wrote to Rollins: "When are you coming in? I feel kinda lonesome. Why not come on up and raise hell with me?"[98] Here is another indication of their closeness: "I note that you expect to be back in New York sometime around now and I needn't

[96]Charles Eberstadt to Clarence Brigham, October 3, 1939. AAS Archives, American Antiquarian Society.

[97]Clarence S. Brigham to Charles Eberstadt, October 9, 1939. AAS Archives, American Antiquarian Society.

[98]Edward Eberstadt to Philip Ashton Rollins, November 14, 1935. Rollins Collection, Princeton University.

tell you how happy I will be to once again clasp your hand and say 'howdee.' Right eagerly I'm a-waiting you."[99]

In the last twenty years of Edward's life, he experienced increasing health difficulties. His health concerned his friends, but some could not resist taking a jab or two at Edward. Eberstadt wrote to Coe, no doubt with a grin: "I had a letter from Bishop Thomas yesterday. He is in Florida and has decided to form a collection on that state. He seemed in gay mood, and waxed downright hilarious over my sorry physical plight. I fear my Floridiana is going to be more expensive than might have been the case had his letter been one of condolence."[100]

Streeter was concerned about his friend's health and recounted to Wagner, "I had a nice visit with Eberstadt about a fortnight ago. He has his eldest son, Lindley in the office now. His health is really very miserable but he certainly is an interesting character and I am very fond of him and give him lots of good advice about taking care of his health which he refuses to follow."[101]

Sometime in early 1934 Edward began to suffer a health problem, which he identified as an "internal hemorrhage," that hindered his ability to work for five weeks while he was confined to bed.[102] He wrote to Philip Rollins about his health: "It begins to look as though I will get 'things' under control and stave off the undertaker after all."[103] Edward continued, "In this regard do you recall your gift to me sometime ago of a bottle of rare old whisky, hoary and mellowed by the passage of time—three-quarters of a century."[104] This was quite a gift—a seventy-five-year-old whisky that had been bottled sometime in the 1860s. Edward continued, "And do you recall your admonition to me—keep this but don't drink it until all hope is abandoned and you feel you are about to die—then call the nurse

---

[99]Edward Eberstadt to Philip Ashton Rollins, September 16, 1937. Rollins Collection, Princeton University.

[100]Edward Eberstadt to W. R. Coe, undated but apparently 1930s. Box 7, Eberstadt Records, Beinecke Library.

[101]Thomas W. Streeter to Henry R. Wagner, June 27, 1933. Box 14, Folder 2, Streeter Papers, American Antiquarian Society.

[102]Edward Eberstadt to Philip Ashton Rollins, January 2, 1934. Rollins Collection, Princeton University.

[103]Edward Eberstadt to Philip Ashton Rollins, January 9, 1934. Rollins Collection, Princeton University.

[104]Ibid.

and bid her feed you one spoonful at a time—it will raise you from your death bed. Well, I still have the bottle and it's still *unopened*."[105]

Actually, the unopened bottle of whisky seems a very remarkable achievement since even Streeter was worried about Edward's health and drinking: "I am getting very much attached to Eberstadt. Though he seems much better I am afraid that he is still a pretty sick man and that he more or less keeps going on whiskey. He wanted to see me yesterday so I cut out my late Friday afternoon bank meeting and instead went out and had a fine talk and four Manhattan cocktails as well."[106] This drinking on Eberstadt's part does not seem too exceptional; Archibald Hanna, the Coe curator at Yale, remembered that Edward in his prime would drink a bottle of bourbon a day.[107]

Henry Wagner was also quite disturbed about Edward's health, especially after Lindley had visited him in Southern California in 1936: "I am quite disturbed about our friend Eberstadt. Lindley talked quite a little bit about him when he was here. He says his father is afraid he has a cancer of the stomach, which seems to be the reason why he will not go to see a doctor. It may be so but I have some doubts about it. More likely he has some ulcerated condition. I wish he would go out to see my doctor."[108]

But Edward was also just as concerned about Wagner's health, as he recounted a dinner party in 1934.

> Well we had quite an exciting time of it at dinner with Mr. Wagner. Just as we finished eating he complained of feeling faint. I called for ice and put it on his head and with fans improvised from the menu cards Mr. Streeter and I went to work. But it was no go—Mr. Wagner was *out*. We spent an hour with him before we could start for his hotel. There we got his physician—old ex-President Theodore Roosevelt's medico—Dr. Lambert. He found Mr. W's blood pressure down below 90 and advised that he go to bed and stay there until further orders—trained nurse in attendance, &c. I left him that night in care of the nurse—next day—despite protests—he got up, dressed,

---

[105]Ibid.

[106]Thomas W. Streeter to Henry R. Wagner, September 16, 1935. Box 14, Folder 2, Streeter Papers, American Antiquarian Society.

[107]As recounted to the author by William Reese, New Haven, Conn., July 2014.

[108]Henry R. Wagner to Thomas W. Streeter, February 25, 1936. Box 14, Folder 3, Streeter Papers, American Antiquarian Society.

phoned me to come over, bade me good bye and started for Washington. If he gets out to you let me know his condition.[109]

Streeter really treasured his time with Edward, as he told Wagner: "I expect to call the old man up in a few minutes now and see how he is getting along. I haven't had a chance to see him now for two or three weeks as the doctor is keeping him very quietly in bed. If anything happens to Ed it is going to take a big chunk out of my life for one of my great pleasures is sitting around and talking with him, not only about books but about everything else."[110]

A few years later Edward was suffering from heart trouble. He added a handwritten note at the end of a letter to Philip and Beulah Rollins: "I just 'dropped down' to see how the boys [Lindley and Charles] were conducting affairs and I cannot resist adding my respects and demands that you get well immediately—Me? I am supposed to be dying of heart trouble now but you know how impossible that would be!"[111]

Edward treasured his friendships—and his joshing—with his customers, as he told Wagner after a visit from Graff. Everett Graff and Wright Howes had just returned from a book-hunting excursion somewhere on the West Coast (apparently to California as the trip included a visit to Wagner), and Edward reported on April 24, 1939: "Today Everett Graff blew into town with the rain and treated me to a long and pleasant chat in re his book junket to the coast. Wright—or wrong—Howes accompanied him as a sort of guide and pilot on the expedition so I imagine the junket yielded considerable junk. Of course Everett set out to make my mouth water, and if I wasn't such a liar myself, I'd have been miserable."[112] The visit with Graff also reminded Edward of his long friendship with Wagner: "Joking all aside, we had a very nice afternoon, much of it

---

[109]Edward Eberstadt to Everett D. Graff, July 3, 1934. Box 4, Folder 2, Graff Papers, Newberry Library.

[110]Thomas W. Streeter to Henry R. Wagner, July 9, 1940. Box 14, Folder 4, Streeter Papers, American Antiquarian Society.

[111]Edward Eberstadt to Beulah Rollins, July 15, 1941. Rollins Collection, Princeton University Library.

[112]Edward Eberstadt to Henry R. Wagner, undated but April 24, 1939; quoted in John Blew, *The Lives and Work of Wright and Zoe Howes*, 258. Graff and Howes took a number of these book hunting trips; Blew reproduces the typed diaries kept by Graff from two of them (fall 1940 and spring 1941) on pages 227–56.

in talking of you. It made me 'homesick' to see you. When do you expect to come east again?"[113]

Sometime in 1939 Edward wrote to Wagner, asking his opinion about his newest—and to date most extravagant—catalogue: "Did you get Catalogue 114, and what did you think of it? I thought it might be my swan song and so decided to go out in a burst of glory. And then to everybody's disappointment I turned around and started to get well."[114] This Eberstadt catalogue had 968 items with extensive descriptions, featuring among other rarities the very rare J. A. Hosmer book on Montana, *A Trip to the States by Way of the Yellowstone and Missouri. With a Table of Distances* (Virginia City, Mont., 1867), priced at $1,650. Wagner did not give out the expected compliment on the catalogue and instead poked his friend Edward about his prices, apparently referring to the Hosmer: "He recently issued a catalogue with the books priced extremely high. I wrote him a letter and said I hoped I would live long enough to see the prices of the books get up to where he put them."[115]

Eberstadt was game to this challenge from Wagner and responded as follows: "Thank you for your appreciative comments on the catalogue. I expect to quote it. It is the first time anyone has admitted that the books they get from me may someday be worth what I charged them. I have always tried to discount not only the future, but the hereafter. Evidently, I'm slipping. I appreciate the tip, however, and shall redouble my efforts to keep well ahead of the coming time."[116]

Henry Wagner was fond of Edward as well; he told Streeter: "I have just had a couple of amusing letters from Ed. Eberstadt. He says he is going to quote my last letter, that in time prices of books may get up to the figures that he puts on them in his last catalogue. Every time I get a letter from him I am regretful that I have not kept a file of his correspondence. It is the most amusing correspondence I have ever indulged with anyone. I mean his side of it."[117]

[113]Edward Eberstadt to Henry R. Wagner, undated but April 24, 1939; quoted in John Blew, *The Lives and Work of Wright and Zoe Howes*, 259.

[114]Edward Eberstadt to Henry R. Wagner, undated but April 24, 1939; quoted in John Blew, *The Lives and Work of Wright and Zoe Howes*, 260.

[115]Henry R. Wagner, *Bullion to Books*, 202.

[116]Ibid.

[117]Henry R. Wagner to Thomas W. Streeter, May 2, 1939. Box 14, Folder 4, Streeter Papers, American Antiquarian Society.

The end of the 1930s marked the survival of Edward Eberstadt through the Depression, the very successful integration of both sons, Lindley and Charles, into the family business, and a strengthening of his close relationships and friendships with his customers. The next two decades would begin with the challenge of World War II (in which Charles would serve) and Edward's increasing health problems, which meant that in the first five years, more of the responsibility for the day-to-day operation of the rare book firm fell upon Lindley's shoulders.

3

The Emergence of the Sons
1940 ✢ 1958

As the country emerged from the Depression, the Eberstadts found themselves facing new challenges. One contribution that both Lindley and Charles brought was the evolution of the standard of scholarship in the catalogues for the rare book firm.

Charles's cataloguing skills were widely known in the trade and among collectors, and his work on the Eberstadt's landmark catalogue, *The Northwest Coast: A Century of Personal Narratives of Discovery, Conquest and Exploration . . . 1741–1841* (1941), even elicited a review in the *New York Times*—still one of the very few rare book catalogues to be so honored. The *Times* noted that the catalogue was "imaginative, intelligent, unorthodox, learned and fascinating to read. Not often does an antiquarian bookseller emerge as a scholar doing independent research and setting the pace for specialists in their own field."[1]

Although there were three Eberstadts working in the business, Edward's increasing health problems and Charles's service during World War II as a U.S. Army lieutenant in the quartermaster corps meant much of the burden for the operation of the rare book firm fell on Lindley during the war years.

Charles had generally assumed responsibility for researching and writing the Eberstadt catalogues, but Lindley proved himself entirely capable of rising to the challenge. In 1943 Lindley wrote catalogue 122, *Indian Captivities and Massacres, Being the Contemporary*

---

[1]Philip Brooks, "Notes on Rare Books," *New York Times* (November 9, 1941), 30.

Record of Caucasian Contact and Conflict with the Native American, which earned an impressive review in the *New York Times*. Lindley described some four hundred rare pamphlets, books, and broadsides. The *Times* wrote that "this illuminating record is one of the best examples of creative cataloguing yet devised by an American dealer. . . . Edward Eberstadt & Sons have set a high standard of scholarship for the American book trade."[2]

At the end of the war, Charles returned to the firm, but although the post–World War II economy was booming, collectors with memories of the recent Depression were wary of rising prices for rare books. Coe was still the Eberstadts' most important customer, but in the postwar boom he still complained when he felt the price for a book was too high. Coe wrote to Edward, "I enclose you a check for $1,000 for the *Banditti of the Rocky Mountains* (Chicago, 1865), which I understand is the net price to you from the Cadmus Book Shop. It is with much reluctance that I have paid this price for the book and particularly in view of the fact that the title page shows it is one of 20,000 copies and also that there are mis-paginations in the book, which to the ordinary mortal would make the book impossible to sell. I am only taking this book on your insistence."[3] But in this case, Eberstadt was right; in spite of the erroneous paginations and the statement of "20th-thousand" printing—which Chicago rare bookseller Wright Howes called "publisher's hyperbole"—this book is actually the earliest account of the vigilantes of Montana and preceded Dimsdale's book on the subject.[4] Besides, no other copy is recorded at auction nor in any bookseller's catalogue.

Edward, as always, had a wry sense of humor and by this time in his life was comfortable poking fun at his own prices, in this case while giving a referral for a customer: "Mr. Heiskell hove in view with a stuffed and crammed wallet and imparted the gladsome news that he was a book collector and wanted all books on Arkansas and the Southwest country. From that day to this I have done my

[2]Philip Brooks, "Notes on Rare Books," *New York Times* (February 21, 1943), 57.

[3]W. R. Coe to Edward Eberstadt, October 21, 1941, Box 10, Eberstadt Records, Beinecke Library.

[4]Wright Howes, *U.S.iana, 1650–1950: A Selective Bibliography in Which Are Described 11,620 Uncommon and Significant Books Relating to the Continental Portion of the United States*, rev. ed. (New York: R. R. Bowker for the Newberry Library, 1962), I-1, 287: "Styled 'twentieth thousand,' obviously a publisher's hyperbole."

best to destroy him financially but since Mr. Heiskell is the owner and editor of the Arkansas Gazette, one of our country's earliest and greatest newspapers, I've never succeeded in even making a dent."[5]

However much customers might wrangle over rare book prices with Edward, they valued their relationship with Eberstadt because he could be relied on for generous as well as humorous advice on values before purchasing a rare book. Clarence S. Brigham, director of the American Antiquarian Society, once wrote asking such a question, and Edward responded: "Thank you for your kind letter of the 13th making inquiry as to a *Chart of the Coast of California* (London, 1854). Yes, I would certainly regard it as a very reasonable buy, indeed, at $10. By all means order it, and after it comes in, gloat over it."[6] Edward was not without his own sense of humor after dispensing this advice: "Enclosed herewith, I am sending you my bill for consultation and advice, fee, $750."[7]

The Chicago collector Everett D. Graff, as president of the Ryerson Steel Company, had a reputation for negotiating better prices from booksellers. Thomas W. Streeter, a savvy businessman himself (chair of the board of Simms Petroleum Corporation and vice-president of the American International Corporation), still took some delight in recounting a story about Graff, of whom he said: "One of the most amusing things happened to my friend, Graff, who is a nice chap but having been in the steel business all his life, is a terrific chiseler." Graff had purchased D. T. Madox's rare work, *Late Account of the Missouri Territory* (Paris, Ky., 1817), Lewis F. Thomas and J. C. Wild, *The Valley of the Mississippi Illustrated* (St. Louis, 1841), and some other choice pieces "at a terribly cheap price."[8] Then Graff thought that the Thomas and Wild, which was illustrated with thirty-four plates, might be incomplete and so wanted to return it. Eberstadt had sold this book to Lathrop Harper, and Harper sold it to the collector Herschel V. Jones. Graff was a careful collator of his books, so his concern about incompleteness is understandable, especially here,

---

[5]Edward Eberstadt to James T. Babb, December 18, 1951. Box 26, Manuscripts and Archives, Yale University Library.

[6]Edward Eberstadt to American Antiquarian Society, February 25, 1944. AAS Archives, American Antiquarian Society.

[7]Ibid.

[8]These books were from the Herschel V. Jones library, which was largely built by the rare bookseller Dr. A. S. W. Rosenbach and dispersed by his firm in the 1940s.

since bookseller and bibliographer Wright Howes notes that this book ends on page 130 with an unfinished sentence and a note that it would be finished in part 10, but that no final part was ever issued.[9]

Philip Rosenbach, brother of Dr. A. S. W. Rosenbach, then came to Harper about the whole matter. Harper said the Wild was fine and he would be glad to take it back. Streeter noted that Philip, "who was very sore at the way Graff had chiseled" one of their employees down on the price, "wired Graff to return the whole lot." Streeter concluded, "Here apparently is a case where chiseling did not pay."[10] However, Graff must have worked out something with Rosenbach, because the Madox book on Missouri is listed in the catalogue of his collection, but the Jones copy of the Thomas and Wild went to the Clements Library.[11]

Streeter was probably exaggerating Graff's reputation for being a cheap buyer; he was a careful buyer, and in reviewing his correspondence, he was more concerned about collation and condition than price. He once consulted Edward regarding a copy of a rare book he had purchased from Dr. Rosenbach. Graff wrote to Eberstadt asking if his copy of Charles King, *The Fifth Cavalry in the Sioux War of 1876* (Milwaukee, 1880) was a good buy at $15. Eberstadt replied: "You will be interested to know that I have checked this up and find that the Doctor purchased this at auction and paid $60 for it. I take it therefore that he mixed up his cost marks when it came to pricing this item. This seems almost tragic—never knew such a thing to happen before in his establishment—perhaps his mind is failing too."[12] Graff replied that "this evens up some high prices on one or two books which Dr. Rosenbach sold me sometime ago. Therefore I will not call his attention to the possible error. I can only add that from all reports this will not ruin Dr. Rosenbach."[13]

Sometime in 1945 Lindley wrote to Everette DeGolyer, who had complained about the price of a rare book: "Dad says in regard to

---

[9]Howes, *U.S.iana*, 580–81.

[10]Thomas W. Streeter to Henry R. Wagner, June 30, 1943. Box 15, Folder 1, Streeter Papers, American Antiquarian Society.

[11]Storm, *A Catalogue of the Everett D. Graff Collection*, 398–99.

[12]Edward Eberstadt to Everett D. Graff, December 3, 1927. Box 4, Folder 3, Graff Papers, Newberry Library.

[13]Edward Eberstadt to Everett D. Graff, December 7, 1927. Box 4, Folder 3, Graff Papers, Newberry Library.

price, take a look at the stock market, particularly on Amerada [the oil company in which DeGolyer had once been president], which Pop says is now selling at well over 150 on a rather ruffled sea. 'Just think,' he says, 'old Dr. Coe is sitting tight up there in the Chrysler building with his 6000 shares bought in the eighties last year.'"[14] The message for the collector DeGolyer was clear if only implied: rare books were good property and worth their price. Even if they seemed high, they were going higher, and Coe, as a canny business-man, knew it.

Some rare book dealers dealt with the lack of pricing knowledge by adopting an auction-like approach. Sam Weller, proprietor of the Zion Book Store in Salt Lake City, once wrote to Coe offering an important Mormon manuscript (not identified in their correspon-dence) in the spring of 1946. Instead of pricing it, he let Coe know that others were considering it and invited him to make an offer.

From the Zion Book Store perspective, this approach seemed to have two important advantages: first, it informed the potential pur-chaser that there was some competition for the piece; and second, that the collector should bid high to be sure of securing it. The unspoken point was to keep the bookseller from making the mistake of pricing a rare item too low. Weller sent the manuscript on approval to Coe, who asked Eberstadt to look it over and decide on an offer. Edward examined it and responded that he thought it "a pretty good piece, I should appraise it at between $350 and $500, but of course don't think it would be wise to so report to the Zion Book Store."[15]

Eberstadt, having seen this maneuver before by booksellers, gamely advised Coe to write the following in reply: "We note that you have quoted this item to certain others and that you have received various bids thereon . . . since you now have bids from other possible players you would be in a position to advise me of the price at which the item could be purchased."[16] Edward knew that this was a very effective counterpoint to the request for a bid on a rare item.

Edward was amused to hear another rare book dealer complain about a collector. One such case was the Los Angeles rare book

[14]Lindley Eberstadt to Everette L. DeGolyer, November 21, 1945. DeGolyer Library.
[15]Edward Eberstadt to W. R. Coe, April 11, 1946. Box 10, Eberstadt Records, Beinecke Library.
[16]Ibid.

dealer Glen Dawson, son of pioneering rare bookseller Ernest Dawson.[17] In 1949 Edward wrote to Henry Wagner, "You gave me a good laugh with your recital of Glen Dawson's contempt for Everett Graff. I was for years the high mucky-muck in the matter of prices; but the new generation has entirely dethroned me."[18] Presumably Graff had attempted to negotiate with the young Glen Dawson on the price of some book Dawson quoted to him, and Wagner had to listen to Dawson vent about it.

Although Eberstadt could happily joke about his own pricing of rare books, it was no laughing matter when the charge of overpricing came from a leading collector and was printed in a book. After Wagner published some rather scathing comments about Eberstadt's pricing in his memoir, *Bullion to Books* (Los Angeles, 1942), he and Edward had a falling out for a couple of years. Later Wagner mentioned the grudge to Streeter: "Speaking of Eberstadt in connection with him reminds to ask you what particular grudge he has against me? I suppose I must have said something in my book about him that he did not like although to tell you the truth I thought I gave him several thousand dollars worth of free advertising."[19]

That is one way of looking at it, but the "several thousand dollars worth of free advertising" included the accusation that Eberstadt overcharged his customers: "The first time that Eberstadt gets a book that looks as if it might be rare he sells it to one of his customers at a big price. Frequently this does not bring any comeback, but occasionally more copies turn up and the book which he thought was rare turns out to be common."[20] This published accusation would probably be more than enough to upset most rare booksellers.

There is a little footnote to this story. Evidently Wagner, ever the hopeful collector, thought that his comments in the book might influence Eberstadt to change his pricing habits. Streeter had written Wagner that Eberstadt had offered him a copy of H. L. W. Leonard's *History of Oregon Territory* (Cleveland, 1846), which he purchased at $850 and offered to Streeter for $1,750. Wagner responded:

[17]Dickinson, *Dictionary of American Antiquarian Bookdealers*, 46–47.

[18]Edward Eberstadt to Henry R. Wagner, December 30, 1949. Box 1, Henry Raup Wagner Papers, Beinecke Library, Yale University.

[19]Henry R. Wagner to Thomas W. Streeter, May 25, 1943. Box 15, Folder 1, Streeter Papers, American Antiquarian Society.

[20]Wagner, *Bullion to Books*, 202.

"Referring to your book of adventures I once looked at the *History of the Oregon Territory* and agree with you that there is nothing to it, but I am rather surprised that Eberstadt wanted to make over 100 per cent profit on the book. I thought he had got over that since *Bullion to Books*."[21] Perhaps Wagner thought the price markup too high, but the book—even if he thought it lacking in content—is noted by Wright Howes in his bibliography as a "dd"—the highest demarcation for extraordinary rarity.[22]

To Streeter, there was a difference, perhaps in spirit or motivation, between chiseling (such as he considered Graff to practice) and good-natured horse-trading. In his negotiations with Edward over prices, one gets the feeling that both enjoyed it. At one point Streeter decided he wanted to purchase the California Declaration of Independence, *En el Puerto de Monterrey de la Alta California* (Monterrey, November 7, 1836), from Eberstadt and another early California printed piece, without of course, tipping his hand. As he told Wagner: "Ed Eberstadt spent the whole day out here yesterday as preliminary dicker for a bunch of my duplicates. I rather think he wants $5000 for the Declaration and the piece which preceded it which is Harding no. 21 [the broadside announcement of the surrender of the Monterrey garrison on November 6, 1836].[23] He says that no. 21 is even more interesting than the Declaration. . . . As a matter of fact, when you consider the prices at which some things are selling nowadays, $5000 doesn't seem out of the way for two such important pieces."[24] Streeter continued with the story: "I have told Ed that though the 'Declaration of Independence' sounds big, the episode was not in fact so very important, but I haven't really read anything to speak of about it yet." Streeter coyly added, "I naturally did not repeat to him your comment, 'I think it is the greatest piece of Californiana that exists.'"[25]

Later Streeter reported a little more about his negotiations with

[21]Henry R. Wagner to Thomas W. Streeter, May 8, 1945. Box 15, Folder 1, Streeter Papers, American Antiquarian Society.

[22]Howes, *U.S.iana*, 340. A copy changed hands in April 2015 for $30,000.

[23]George L. Harding, "A Census of California Spanish Imprints, 1833–1845," *California Historical Quarterly* 12 (June 1933), 125–36.

[24]Thomas W. Streeter to Henry R. Wagner, February 2, 1946. Box 15, Folder 1, Streeter Papers, American Antiquarian Society.

[25]Ibid.

Eberstadt. "I haven't yet got the Declaration of Independence (California, 1836) or the piece that went with it, for Eberstadt has been laid up with the flu. He says he will either be well or dead by next week, and I am betting he is going to live. It will probably take quite a while for me to buy the two pieces, for he can't help knowing that I want them, and he gets a lot of pleasure out of negotiating."[26] Streeter finally did end up with both California broadsides: the November 6 announcement of the surrender brought $1,800 at the Parke-Bernet Sale of his collection in 1968, and the November 7 Declaration of Independence brought $4,500.[27]

Even if Streeter sometimes felt that Eberstadt overcharged him, he still felt there were advantages to the relationship. "Every now and then, I probably pay Ed much too much for books but I am sure I am one of his favored customers and I get a first chance at many items, and that is worth a lot in this game, and I do think Ed has a lot more pleasure in selling books to me than Coe for I usually know what it is all about and he doesn't have to struggle with me over price, for I either pay what he asks or I don't buy the piece at all."[28]

When Archibald Hanna was selected as the curator for the Coe Collection in 1952, he made a good impression on Edward Eberstadt, who wrote to the Yale head librarian, James T. Babb: "I also want to say at this time, how wonderfully your judgment in the selection of Arch Hanna has been justified. He wears well. Every time I see him, I come away better impressed with the very rapid progress he is making, not only as to his information on western books, but also as a salesman of the library and Yale."[29]

Lindley also wrote a personal note to Hanna about his selection: "Just got the official word on your selection as Curator and Librarian of the Coe & Mason Collections [the Mason was an important Benjamin Franklin collection]. That is wonderful news and I think everyone is entitled to congratulations—Yale, Mason, Coe, Babb

---

[26]Thomas W. Streeter to Henry R. Wagner, February 20, 1946. Box 15, Folder 1, Streeter Papers, American Antiquarian Society.

[27]Parke-Bernet Galleries, *The Celebrated Collection of Americana Formed by the Late Thomas Winthrop Streeter* (New York: Parke-Bernet Galleries, 1968), numbers 2481–82.

[28]Thomas W. Streeter to Henry R. Wagner, December 21, 1949. Box 15, Folder 2, Streeter Papers, American Antiquarian Society.

[29]Edward Eberstadt to James T. Babb, March 11, 1953, Box 26, Manuscripts and Archives, Yale University Library.

THE EMERGENCE OF THE SONS 99

& of course you. If we can ever help just say the word."[30] Hanna responded to Lindley: "Thank you for your kind note. Needless to say I am more thrilled than anyone over the appointment."[31] He would go on to have a distinguished career of nearly thirty years as Yale's Coe Curator of Western Americana.

Archibald Hanna did not let the congratulatory remarks from the Eberstadts distract him from watching prices. Although Edward slowed down somewhat in the rare book business after 1950, Lindley and Charles increasingly had to answer the same charges of over-pricing books from collectors and curators. At one point, Hanna thought the price too high ($400) for a set of six broadsides dealing with the fur trade from the Hudson's Bay Company in catalogue 130. "We are not happy about the price of number 233, thinking it way too much for us to pay."[32]

Charles took the awkward responsibility of responding to Hanna's charge of high prices in the catalogue: "I only mention this as some sort of explanation as to why we are unable to do any better on the other list, which Mr. Hanna thought might be overpriced. Actually, although the prices often seem high, there are so many factors considered in running a business such as time and salaries, and over-head, not to mention travelling and the original cost of each item, that in many cases there is not much room. I have heard the impression given that we are waxing fat on this business, but, believe me, it just ain't so. And at the end of the year it always works out that there has been very little in it beyond the bare living for any of us."[33]

Edward might have had this incident with the charge of high prices in mind when he later wrote to Hanna enclosing a mimeo-graph quote of two court records dealing with the Missouri Mor-mon war from the Kansas City bookseller, Frank Glenn, with this aside: "Whenever you get to thinking that Old Man Eberstadt is expensive, just take a look at this and revise your opinion. Frank

---

[30]Lindley Eberstadt to Archibald Hanna, September 25, 1952. Curatorial Files, Beinecke Library.

[31]Archibald Hanna to Lindley Eberstadt, October 1, 1952. Curatorial Files, Beinecke Library.

[32]James T. Babb to Edward Eberstadt & Sons, July 31, 1952. Curatorial Files, Beinecke Library.

[33]Charles Eberstadt to James T. Babb, July 30, 1953. Box 26, Manuscripts and Archives, Yale University Library.

Glenn just offered this to us and at the special price to us as dealers of ten thousand smackers! wow!"[34]

Of course, a curator might have a different perspective on the value of a rare pamphlet. Consider the experience that Edward had when he sent Hanna a quote for a rare pamphlet, Lucius Vermilya's *The Battles of Mexico from the Beginnings to the End of the War, with a Sketch of California* (Prattsville, Ohio, 1849), complete with the original printed wrappers for $500 in 1954. Archibald was not enthusiastic about the pamphlet; as he told Edward, "the fact that we already have a copy detracts in some aspects from its excessive rarity. However, you will be pleased to know that our copy lacks the wrappers. What I want to know of course is how much it will cost me to exchange my copy for yours?"[35] From Hanna's perspective, the library would consider having a complete copy—if the price were reasonable.

But from an antiquarian bookseller's perspective of dealing with collectors, it was a case of completely different items. Edward took a tutorial air in responding to Hanna's implied assertion that a copy without the wrappers was in any way equivalent in rarity to a copy with the original printed wrappers:

> Now to get back to the Vermilya, I note that you quote my appraisement of it, wherein, after a few hefty snorts of old Dr. Griddley's Pain killer and snake-bite remedy, I characterized the piece as "an advanced collector's item of purest ray supreme," Archie, sit back and listen to the old professor. The fact that you have a copy which lacks the printed wrappers in no way alters my comment. A rarity of this caliber must be perfect or it just isn't a copy. It is a cripple and an annoyance—a Lillian Russell sans teeth. More particularly is this the case in the present instance, for it is on the wrapper only that the vital words "with a glance at California" appear. This is vastly more than a mere bibliographic "point." . . . With that thought in mind I will reduce the asking price to $250 and your copy, asking you to please have a sharp photograph made to size, of the front and back wrappers.[36]

[34]Edward Eberstadt to Archibald Hanna, January 21, 1957. Curatorial Files, Beinecke Library.

[35]Archibald Hanna to Edward Eberstadt, March 9, 1954. Curatorial Files, Beinecke Library.

[36]Edward Eberstadt to Archibald Hanna, March 11, 1954. Curatorial Files, Beinecke Library.

Perhaps the Eberstadts had another customer in mind for this imperfect copy, since it does not appear in their later catalogues. Edward's tutorial notwithstanding, Hanna did not hesitate to comment when he thought the price in an Eberstadt catalogue needed adjusting.

Sometimes at auction collectors can be their own worst competitor, especially when a bit of biblio-paranoia sets in. In this case, Everett Graff was aware of Streeter's close relationship to Eberstadt. Perhaps Edward had asked Graff about carrying some bids for him at the C. G. Littell sale in 1945, a highly anticipated auction of some important rare western books. (Littell was a Chicago book collector and president of the R. R. Donnelley Printing Company.)[37] Before the auction, Streeter relayed a bit of gossip about Graff's strategy to Wagner: "Ed Eberstadt told me that Graff called him up from Chicago the other day and said he had a nice visit with you. The Littell books are going to be sold in January and Graff is coming on the sale to bid for himself. He doesn't trust Eberstadt or Harper and thinks I have an inside track with them."[38] This may not have been far-fetched, since Streeter considered both men to be close friends and confidants of his collecting. As it happened, Graff may have been playing coy with Streeter; he had actually already arranged to have Eberstadt carry his bids at the Littell sale, as Edward wrote to Graff after the auction: "I'm glad you decided to have me represent you. I did the best I could and I hope the results prove me to be a fairly good 'Man Friday.'"[39]

In the early spring of 1954 the Eberstadts began plotting regularly with the Yale curators on the William J. Holliday auction at Parke-Bernet Galleries. (Yale was interested in having the Eberstadts bid for them on about fifty items.)[40] Holliday was a steel industrialist from Indiana with a home in Tucson, Arizona (his son was the western historian J. S. Holliday).[41] One of the high spots in this

---

[37]Dickinson, *Dictionary of American Book Collectors*, 207–208.

[38]Thomas W. Streeter to Henry R. Wagner, December 12, 1944. Box 15, Folder 1, Streeter Papers, American Antiquarian Society.

[39]Edward Eberstadt to Everett D. Graff, February 12, 1945. Box 3, Folder 15, Graff Papers, Newberry Library. See also "Rare Book Brings $1,000," *New York Times* (February 7, 1945), 19.

[40]Parke-Bernet Galleries, *Western Americana, Many of Great Rarity. The Distinguished Collection Formed by W. J. Holliday* . . . (New York: Parke-Bernet Galleries, 1954).

[41]Dickinson, *Dictionary of American Book Collectors*, 166–67; and David Magee, "The W. J. Holliday Sale of Western Americana," *Quarterly Newsletter of the Book Club of California* 19 (Summer 1954), 60–64.

sale was Granville Stuart's *Montana As It Is* (New York, 1865), with the rare large folding map, which brought $2,200.[42] Edward also attended this sale, testifying to his continued interest and participation in the firm during the 1950s. Edward also made it a point to purchase a favorite rare book of his at the Holliday sale—John L. Campbell's *Idaho: Six Months in the New Gold Diggings* (Chicago, 1864) for $400—the guide to the Montana gold rush that he had handled a number of times was always a favorite of his.

After the Holliday sale, Hanna wrote to Charles: "I want to thank you and Lin for your hospitality on Wednesday. It was certainly a most exciting occasion, although I am ready to join with you in organizing a society for the suppression of Glen Dawson. Did anyone ever find out the name of his client? I suppose we should not be greedy but it was a bit annoying."[43] Hanna was referring to a major new collector, Kenneth Bechtel; Los Angeles rare book dealer Glen Dawson was executing his bids at the sale. (Bechtel was one of the founders of the Bechtel Construction Company and national president of the Boy Scouts of America from 1956 to 1959.)

This curiosity on Hanna's—and no doubt the Eberstadts'—part is natural in the atmosphere of rare books, where gossip seems to be a form of oxygen needed for survival. Streeter also had heard that the new collector, Bechtel, was spending so much money on rare books that Warren Howell would not give even another collector Bechtel's address when asked for it politely. Bechtel, however, wanted to meet Streeter, and Howell reluctantly made the arrangements.

Streeter told Wagner how he intended to have his own bit of fun: "I am quite certain that he [Bechtel] is also on Glen Dawson's list of favored clients, so just to make the whole thing more interesting all around, I am asking Ed out here for this coming weekend, and not asking either Howell or Dawson."[44] Eberstadt was probably tickled to have the opportunity to privately meet an important new client

---

[42]"1865 Book Brings $2,200," *New York Times* (April 23, 1954), 24. "The most cherished Montana book," according to Howes, *U.S.iana*, 565.

[43]Archibald Hanna to Charles Eberstadt, April 26, 1954. Curatorial Files, Beinecke Library. Also same, April 30, 1954: "The books purchased by Mr. Beinecke and Mr. Coe arrived safely and I am now gloating over them. Thinking back to the tense situation during the auction I am sure you earned your commission."

[44]Thomas W. Streeter to Henry R. Wagner, October 13, 1947. Box 15, Folder 2, Streeter Papers, American Antiquarian Society.

of another rare bookseller. It was due to his friendship with an old client of his own, Streeter, who didn't mind helping him.

Despite their best plotting, dealers such as the Eberstadts did not always get what they were competing for at auction, even if they were bidding for a retail customer. On December 12, 1956, an auction in New York had a copy of William Hamilton and Samuel Irvin, *An Ioway Grammar* (Ioway and Sac Mission Press, Indian Territory, 1848).[45] Lindley wrote to Archibald that day:

> I very much regret to report to you that we were unsuccessful in obtaining the Ioway Grammar on which you gave me a bid in today's sale. I exceeded your bid by $100 and still didn't get it so I think we can feel more or less that we gave it everything it was entitled to and I am relatively certain when and if another one comes along we can get it a great deal cheaper. I suppose one of the first things one must become reconciled to in this game is that one can't get everything. . . . Truly, I think we should not feel bad at losing this at the price it brought, $625.[46]

For most books, that statement about a cheaper copy might be true, but for this little rarity no other copy appeared at auction until it returned decades later. It seems that the New York rare book dealer John Fleming bought this copy, which he sold to the great collector of Native American linguistics, Dr. Frank Siebert, in 1962.

Of course, collecting goes both ways. Charles Eberstadt, following his father's canny tactics, was happy to let Hanna know when his rival, Dr. Siebert, missed something too. In October 1958 Charles wrote to Hanna that item 174 from catalogue 147 (a Spanish colonial manuscript journal of a trip through Texas) was his, and that "Doc Siebert" had just called for it, but had been told it was sold.[47]

Collectors sometimes changed their interests—some like Vandale quitting his Texas collection and starting a new collecting interest in the fur trade. In this regard, Coe—the Eberstadts' most important customer for decades—increasingly became less interested in sheer rarity for the sake of collectability and, as his collection was

---

[45]For bibliographic information, see Storm, *A Catalogue of the Everett D. Graff Collection*, 261 (where it is number 1757).

[46]Lindley Eberstadt to Archibald Hanna, December 12, 1956. Curatorial Files, Beinecke Library.

[47]This item was an important manuscript of a Spanish colonial account of a trip through Texas.

being transferred to Yale in the 1940s, more concerned with research value for scholars and historians. After one such offering, he wrote to Edward: "For your guidance—I am not particularly interested in acquiring at considerable expense, items that can only be judged by their extreme rarity or by the fact that no one else has them, that is, unless they are of real value to scholars and research."[48] As a result, Coe increasingly added rare manuscripts and archives of original sources of western history to his collection—much to the later benefit of Yale and numerous other scholars.

Even late in the collecting career of Coe, Edward still liked to tout the relative importance of recent acquisitions. After Coe agreed in May 1949 to purchase books that Eberstadt called "cornerstone books" for his collection, Coe took a jab at Edward, replying: "In respect to your statement that I have acquired three of the 'cornerstone' books in my library—if this designation keeps up the library will consist of nothing but cornerstones."[49] Despite Coe's good-natured complaining, the same letter also enclosed a $9,000 check for the books.

The Eberstadts sometimes found they were offering an item to a customer who had previously been offered the same piece at a lower price by the Eberstadts' source. Edward wrote offering a California Gold Rush letter to Yale as follows: "Dear Archie, Sit back and hold on. Having just secured and am sending on to you, under separate cover, to gloat over with me, one of the earliest and most interesting accounts of the Gold Discovery and Rush that has ever come our way."[50] The curator's prick to the bookseller's balloon came when Hanna replied, "The fact is I turned down the Warner letter on the California gold discoveries when it was offered to me at one-half the price it has now attained."[51] There is no need of documentation to visualize the pained look that must have appeared on Edward's face.

On occasion a librarian or collector will see a rare book in a bookseller's catalogue and know not only which auction it came from

[48]W. R. Coe to Edward Eberstadt, September 23, 1954. Box 11, Eberstadt Records, Beinecke Library.

[49]W. R. Coe to Edward Eberstadt, May 18, 1949. Box 10, Eberstadt Records, Beinecke Library.

[50]Edward Eberstadt to Archibald Hanna, January 18, 1957. Curatorial Files, Beinecke Library.

[51]Archibald Hanna to Edward Eberstadt, January 21, 1957. Curatorial Files, Beinecke Library.

but how much was paid for it. Charles wrote to Clarence Brigham of the American Antiquarian Society offering a copy of the Alonso DeCalves, *Travels to the Westward* (Portland, Maine, 1796). Dr. Brigham offered a perfect example of how to make a counteroffer without making a counteroffer. To Charles he wrote, "Ordinarily we should be inclined to take the Portland, 1796 edition of DeCalves. I was the underbidder on this item at a Parke-Bernet Sale in 1945, when it went for $60. . . . I don't believe in making counter-offers, but would merely say that if it came up for sale, we should not bid over $100 for it."[52] Charles was gracious enough to reduce his price and was glad to accept "your carefully couched offer of $100."[53] This is pricing diplomacy in its very finest form.

A temptation for booksellers, including Charles, when cataloguing a book for sale, is the tantalizing assertion, "only known copy." Sometimes it is the final *pièce de résistance* applied to a sexy object for the collection; more often it is used to dress up an otherwise unimportant piece of merchandise. A letter written by Streeter is revealing in this aspect. After Edward wrote his article touting the highlights of the Coe Collection for the Yale Library *Gazette* at the time of Coe's gift, Streeter wrote him: "I think you have done a swell job. . . . I got a great kick out of some of your lines, such as the one on page 55 'that charmed, but never-quite-assured realm of the only known copy.' When I helped put on the New York Public Library *Texas Exhibition* in 1936, I stubbed my toe once or twice on the 'only known copy' business and have used that phrase with great caution ever since."[54] Edward, of course, had first learned that lesson the hard way back in 1922 with his experience in touting the Stephen F. Austin *Esposicion* (Mexico City, 1835) as "one of two known copies" and had had the book returned from Anderson Galleries.

Besides the risk of the "only known copy," another potential cataloguing hazard was the occasional but inevitable typesetting error. Charles wrote of a particularly egregious one that slipped into their new catalogue 133 (published in 1954): "The proofs are very rough,

---

[52]Clarence Brigham to Charles Eberstadt, July 15, 1948. Archives, American Antiquarian Society.

[53]Clarence Brigham to Charles Eberstadt, July 21, 1948. Archives, American Antiquarian Society.

[54]Thomas W. Streeter to Edward Eberstadt, October 6, 1948. Box 10, Eberstadt Records, Beinecke Library.

but that will not interfere with the checking. Among the 'typos' I noticed a lulu—item 183, a Donner party book that the printer has listed under *Dinner Party!* Grisly unconscious humor."[55] Unconscious, perhaps, but Charles did not correct the proofs and retained the "grisly humor" for the published catalogue. Charles also had his own deliberate fun in the catalogues. In catalogue 123, for John G. Bourke's *The Urine Dance of the Zuni Indians of New Mexico* (Ann Arbor, Mich., 1885), Charles wrote the following description (with a racist flourish typical in 1947): "We can't ascertain whether these zany Zunis were cliff-dwellers or lived in pepees [*sic*], but in any case they were obviously not house-broken."[56]

The Eberstadt catalogues were always an informative and even delightful read; even a collector like Coe, who had given his western Americana collection to Yale in 1948, could still pore over an Eberstadt catalogue in 1952 and pick out over sixty items that he wanted to talk to Lindley about to add to his collection at Yale.[57]

It had long been apparent that there was a need for a new edition of the Wagner-Camp bibliography, *The Plains and the Rockies*, to correct errors and add items the compilers had missed. There was some discussion about Charles editing the new third edition. This was not entirely unexpected as Charles's work on the landmark Eberstadt *Northwest Coast* catalogue was widely heralded, as was his bibliographic knowledge.

However, Wagner was categorically opposed to the idea of using Charles Eberstadt. At one point, Streeter may have tested the waters on behalf of Charles and apparently suggested that Eberstadt might be a good editor for the new edition. Wagner responded with a definite distain: "I suppose you might suggest that Charlie Eberstadt would do it, but I would never agree to that, if I had anything to say about it. I have never yet had any bookseller have anything to do

---

[55]Charles Eberstadt to James T. Babb, November 8, 1953. Curatorial Files, Beinecke Library.

[56]Edward Eberstadt & Sons, *Americana Catalogue 123* (New York, 1947), item 21.

[57]Among the rarities Coe selected from the Eberstadt catalogue 131 were numbers 95, *Lieutenant Butler's Report of His Journey from Fort Garry to the Rocky Mountain House* (Ottawa, 1871; $450)—a rare Canadian overland to the Rockies; 105, a broadside printing of the *Columbia District Mining Laws from Gold Rush California* (1853; $200); 107, an archive of 36 California Gold Rush letters (1851–55; $450); and 195, H. W. Holmes, an unrecorded map of Kansas and the Colorado gold regions (Philadelphia, 1859; $450).

with any of my books and I do not propose to start now. If Charlie Eberstadt wants to write a Supplement, or Additions and Corrections, as a separate work that would be quite sufficient in my opinion and infinitely cheaper."[58] Wagner, as ever, was blind to his own shortcomings as a scholar, claiming, for example, that *The Plains and the Rockies* had never been more than a list of books he owned or hoped to acquire, not a comprehensive work.

In hindsight, it is a shame that the third edition of Wagner-Camp did not have the benefit of Charles Eberstadt's scholarship and attention to detail, especially since Camp made some substantial changes that only made the third edition even more of a hodge-podge of inconsistent information. On the other hand, Charles never came close to realizing any rigorous scholarly project. The press of work in the firm, and the too frequent reliance on the bottle—the bane of the father and the sons—did not allow it.

Many critical comments were made about the new third edition.[59] J. S. ("Jack") Holliday, a rising western historian (who later wrote a best-selling book, *The World Rushed In*, about the California Gold Rush), wrote to W. F. Kelleher, a rare book dealer in New Jersey with many western interests: "Jesus K-Rist! What a job of book making! Please turn to page 600 in this cheaply gotten up Wagner-Camp and note the index skips from Whipple to Wyeth. There is a whole column left out, containing such unimportant items as Marcus Whitman, George Wilkes. . . . Get after that Long outfit [the publishers in Columbus, Ohio] and tell them to get out some sort of a supplementary sheet that we can stub into the index of the bibliography, as the book is utterly worthless without an accurate index."[60]

Edward reported to James Babb, head librarian at Yale, about the new Wagner-Camp bibliography as well:

> I have had a talk with Everett Graff on the phone with regard to the Wagner-Camp. He felt very much as I do about the work and had no hesitancy in *orally* damning the work. And in today's mail he has

[58]Henry R. Wagner to Thomas W. Streeter, July 21, 1947. Box 15, Folder 2, Streeter Papers, American Antiquarian Society.

[59]Charles L. Camp, ed., *Henry R. Wagner's The Plains and the Rockies: A Bibliography of Original Narratives of Travel and Adventure, 1800–1865* (Columbus, Ohio: Long's College Book Company, 1953); it is a poorly printed and bound volume.

[60]J. S. Holliday to Wm. F. Kelleher, August 5, 1953. Box 26, Manuscripts and Archives, Yale University Library.

written me about it: "After our telephone conversation I took a look at the latest edition of the Wagner-Camp, which I had not looked at for some weeks, and I am sorry to find that I never went entirely through the book, but you will find a number of corrections and comments in the margin, which I hope you can decipher. Those entries I have checked yielded many mistakes."[61]

Charles wrote about the new edition to Hanna: "The new Wagner-Camp is a great disappointment to us and shows far too clearly what slip-shod work the editor consistently did. I can think of no possible excuse for his treatment of the Coe Collection because he spent a week up there with you and a week here with us and was thoroughly apprised of all the items that should have been located in the Coe Collection, but apparently in one of his wilder moments he seems to have thrown these notes skyward."[62]

For example, Camp describes the Coe copy of Wagner-Camp 391, the Hewitt Northwest overland printed in Olympia in 1863 (the same copy acquired from Skiff), as incomplete; just to make sure it wasn't, they had Hanna check on it. He reported, "I have checked Camp's notes in the new edition of *The Plains and the Rockies* on Hewitt. The Hewitt, which he says is imperfect, is in almost mint condition. According to the collation he gives it is perfect. . . . Either he did not look at the book at all or else he mislaid his notes and relied on memory, for the statement is absurd and untrue."[63]

Still, after Charles had a chance to review the book he wrote, "Bad as the new book (Wagner-Camp) looks ('horribly printed')—and is—it nevertheless contains a heck of a lot of new information and titles."[64] And of course later on, the errors went the other way too, favoring Coe with the only known copy. Lindley wrote to Hanna in November 1953, "Do you have a copy of Wagner-Camp 326B?[65] Seems to me that I showed the only one I ever saw to Charlie Camp

[61]Edward Eberstadt to James T. Babb, August 10, 1953. Box 26, Manuscripts and Archives, Yale University Library.

[62]Charles Eberstadt to Archibald Hanna, June 29, 1953. Curatorial Files, Beinecke Library.

[63]Archibald Hanna to Edward Eberstadt, September 14, 1953. Curatorial Files, Beinecke Library.

[64]Charles Eberstadt to James T. Babb, August 14, 1953. Box 26, Manuscripts and Archives, Yale University Library.

[65]This book was an anonymous German account, *Ein Ritt nach Californien*, of a trip to California through the Southwest.

and I guess he assumed it was in the Coe Collection, as I note it is listed as being in Coe. If you do not have it, I had better sell it to Mr. Coe, and reduce by one, the errors in the new bibliography."[66] Hanna wrote back that they did not have this German account of an overland journey across the Mormon trail into California, which was published in 1859. In any event, Camp eventually privately circulated a seven-page typed carbon list with well over a hundred corrections for the bibliography.[67]

The Eberstadts knew that competition between collectors is a constant part of the rare book collecting game. Of course, it is even sweeter from the collector's point of view when he acquires something desperately wanted by another collector. Streeter had known for some time that Coe's collection lacked only one of the eight known imprints from the Nez Perce Mission press in early Idaho, which was the so-called "Lapwai laws," *Wilupupki 1842, Lapwai* (Clearwater, Id., 1842). When he acquired a copy, he was beside himself with glee. Streeter bragged a bit to Wagner: "The big news with me in the book line is that I have just bought from Mike Walsh of Goodspeed's the Lapwai Laws, printed at Clearwater, Idaho, on the mission press in 1842."[68] Streeter continued gloating to Wagner:

> This is the only one of the eight Lapwai imprints that Coe lacks, and I am mean enough to think it the most important. A year or so ago Ed told me that the librarian of Whitman College had been on a visit east, and he had a great time plying him with liquor and offering him a huge sum for the *Laws.* Coe said he would pay up to $10,000 for them. Anyway, I now have them and we have checked up with Whitman College to make sure their copy is safely in their book vault. This copy came from some little institutional library in Massachusetts. I haven't told Ed about it yet as I only learned last week that the Whitman College copy was OK.[69]

---

[66]Lindley Eberstadt to Archibald Hanna, November 13, 1953. Curatorial Files, Beinecke Library.

[67]Charles L. Camp, typed carbon list: "Additions and Corrections. Plains and Rockies. 3rd Ed. 1953," 7 pages. Copy of Edward Eberstadt & Sons, now belonging to Michael D. Heaston, Wichita, Kansas; presumably these typed carbon lists were circulated to booksellers, collectors, and curators.

[68]Thomas W. Streeter to Henry R. Wagner, August 27, 1951. Box 15, Folder 4, Streeter Papers, American Antiquarian Society.

[69]Thomas W. Streeter to Henry R. Wagner, August 27, 1951. Box 15, Folder 4, Streeter Papers, American Antiquarian Society.

Mike Walsh choosing to sell the book to Streeter demonstrates some of the idiosyncrasies of the rare book game. Walsh in 1928 had vastly underpriced one of the Nez Perce mission imprints in a Goodspeed's catalogue. The Americana bookseller Charles Everitt recalled about that earlier copy: "I can comfort myself by remembering what befell my almost infallible friend Mike Walsh of Goodspeed's. His catalogue 168 was among the most interesting I have ever seen. In the midst of looking through it I picked up the telephone and called Boston. 'Mike, have you still got 2211?' 'No, sorry it's gone. How much did I slip on that?' 'Plenty,' said I, reluctantly hanging up."[70]

That rare book was *The Nez Perce's First Book*, and Walsh would have known that the Eberstadts were seeking to complete a collection for Coe of the Nez Perce Mission imprints. Nevertheless, Walsh chose to sell it to Streeter rather than to the Eberstadts.[71] This is one of the times when chance and relationship comes into play in the rare book game—choosing where to offer a particular copy of a rarity for sale, and in this case choosing a collector like Streeter rather than a competing dealer like Eberstadt.

Even though Edward missed the copy of the Lapwai laws that went to Streeter, he did not give up on acquiring the Nez Perce imprint. Edward later wrote to the Yale librarian, James Babb (who also hoped to acquire the rare imprint): "Lindley has left on his long trip and I am wondering if perhaps you and he will meet in Walla Walla. I think he took his shotgun with him, and if we don't get the Nez Perce Laws there is going to be a dead librarian out thatta way."[72] Unfortunately for the Eberstadts, Lindley was not successful in acquiring this final imprint until Streeter's copy came up for sale in 1968.

Edward just as often was the winner in the competition for rare books. He wrote to a New York City collector of overland guidebooks that he had just acquired copies of two Colorado Gold Rush books: Redpath and Hinton, *Handbook to Kansas Territory and the Rocky Mountains* (New York, 1859), and Charles M. Clark, *A Trip to Pike's Peak* (Chicago, 1861), from the New York dealer Adolph

---

[70]Everitt, *The Adventures of a Treasure Hunter*, 168.

[71]This book was sold in the October 23, 1968, Streeter sale (number 3296, bringing $4,000).

[72]Edward Eberstadt to James Babb, January 27, 1950. Box 10, Eberstadt Records, Beinecke Library.

Stager (proprietor of Cadmus Rare Books). Neither book is particularly rare, but the greater pleasure for Eberstadt was "I just nailed it at the psychological moment when our other very dear mutual friend, Peter Decker [a New York dealer of rare Americana],[73] was frantically wiring Adolph for it. So you see, I have already had quite some pleasure out of it."[74] The pleasure was greater for Eberstadt because Peter Decker—who had an office very close to his—was agent at this time for the very wealthy collector Frederick W. Beinecke.

Frederick W. Beinecke would become an important Eberstadt customer. He was part of the family-owned Sperry and Hutchinson (S&H Green Stamps) and began a collection of western Americana with Peter Decker as his agent in the late 1940s. Together with his brother, Edwin J. Beinecke (E. J., who collected Robert Louis Stevenson, Samuel Johnson, and medieval illuminated manuscripts), and his son, William Beinecke (who did not collect rare books), they built the Beinecke Rare Book Library at Yale, and both F. W. and E. J. contributed their collections.[75]

Edward later recounted a great missed opportunity to purchase one of the treasures of western Americana—the original manuscript map of the Lewis and Clark expedition, which was owned by a descendant, Julia Clark Voorhis, and not in the Library of Congress or some other institution. As Edward recounts it, "I damn near fainted when I read of the maps, for at that time, Mrs. Julia Clark Voorhis, who owned them and was a distant relative of my mother's, lived at the Hotel Bonta and occupied an apartment adjoining my mother's. We three used to hob-nob together in those dimly distant

[73]Peter Decker was a leading New York City rare book dealer specializing in Americana; he also had an office next to Edward Eberstadt's (55 W. 42nd Street) at 51 W. 42nd Street. See also Donald C. Dickinson, *Dictionary of American Antiquarian Bookdealers*, 47–48; see also the three-volume set, *Peter Decker's Catalogues of Americana* (Austin: William Reese, 1979), which contain a long and useful reminiscence by Peter Decker.

[74]Edward Eberstadt to A. H. Greenly, Esq., August 19, 1946. Box 10, Eberstadt Records, Beinecke Library.

[75]For more on Frederick William Beinecke, see Dickinson, *Dictionary of American Book Collectors*, 32–33; Archibald Hanna, "Frederick W. Beinecke, 1887–1971," *Yale Library Gazette* 45 (October 1971), 65–66; "Frederick Beinecke, 84, Dead," *New York Times* (August 1, 1971), 53. For more on Edwin John Beinecke, see Donald C. Dickinson, *Dictionary of American Book Collectors*, 31–32; Herbert W. Liebert and Thomas E. Marston, "The Edwin J. Beinecke Memorial Collection," *Yale Library Gazette* 44 (October 1970), 37–52; "Edwin John Beinecke Dies at 84; Headed Sperry and Hutchinson," *New York Times* (January 22, 1970), 37.

days, and I, because of the situation and the decorum involved, and doubtless my extreme youth, could not bring myself to besmirch our acquaintanceship with so crass a matter as the purchase of the dear lady's historical material. Holy God!"[76] This great map was purchased by Frederick Beinecke via the Old Print Shop in New York and is one of the treasures in the Beinecke Library today.

Even the great collector of Texana, Earl Vandale, couldn't keep out of the rare book game. After he sold his collection to the University of Texas, he had resolved to quit collecting. But soon he wrote to the Eberstadts: "Dear Friends, Now that the labor and close application of checking, packing and shipping my bunch of books (estimated at some 8,000 books) to the University of Texas is over, I am at a loss as to what to do." Vandale decided to start collecting "some mountain men and fur trade items. My reasoning for this is that it did not last too long and the books written about [it] are not too numerous."[77] Ah, the famous last words of many a collector starting a new venture—the subject is not too vast and the books therefore must be few!

Vandale added one more qualifier to the Eberstadts, which will be obvious to someone with years of collecting experience. "Then too, if I would restrict my purchases to extra fine copies that should keep down the labor and hustle of rapid buying."[78] Instead of accumulating another large book collection, Vandale would concentrate on beautiful copies of rare books. Many beginning collectors are tempted by relatively inexpensive but also incomplete copies of rare books. Eberstadt advised one collector: "As you no doubt know, the value of rare books depends largely on their completeness and condition. Poor copies are a poor investment, but imperfect ones are money entirely thrown away."[79] Vandale's and Eberstadt's are wise words of advice for any collector, usually learned only through extensive and expensive personal experience.

---

[76]Edward Eberstadt to James T. Babb, May 14, 1952. Box 26, Manuscripts and Archives, Yale University Library.

[77]Earl Vandale to Edward Eberstadt, January 24, 1948. Vandale Papers, Nita Stewart Haley Memorial Library.

[78]Ibid.

[79]The cross-checking of pages, plates, and maps in a copy with an entry in a standard bibliography. Variants don't always mean incompleteness, since it might also indicate another previously unknown issue of the work. But if it is missing plates or pages or a map that should be there, then it is incomplete.

Charles responded to this news of Vandale's renewed collecting with hearty congratulations: "I think you are selecting one of the most interesting of all the specialties of Western History in determining to form a collection of the fur trade and fur trappers." Charles later added: "We heard about your retiring some months ago and extend hearty felicitations; we heard about your selling your collection and extend regretful commiserations; and now we hear about you starting up again and extend all congratulations. I hope this will be the beginning of the beautiful friendship we once had and as proof of our sincerity please note the enclosed certificate."[80]

The "Matrimonial Certificate" was printed in Dallas County, Texas, in the 1870s; Charles filled it in so that it unites Earl Vandale and Edward Eberstadt & Sons, if not in matrimony at least in the pursuit of holy book collecting.[81]

Later, Charles, ever the hopeful bookseller, sent Vandale a shipment on approval of a number of books he had asked about; Vandale, however, stuck to his collecting plan. Most of the books were not in the fine condition he wanted, and he returned the books to the Eberstadts with the following explanation: "What I am trying to do is just build up a bunch of superfine copies and condition is the main thing, not the ownership of a copy of an item."[82] The search for rare items in fine condition is a good objective for collectors, if not always for booksellers like the Eberstadts who were always eager to move some inventory.

Files of early newspapers from boomtowns on the frontier are among the rarest and most difficult sources to obtain for the history of the West. Many of these preserve the only notices of historical events in their communities. Edward had an affinity for these runs of early western newspapers; while working on the Coe appraisal of the Yale gift, he once remarked on the rarity of the *Rocky Mountain News* (Denver, 1859–60) to the Yale librarian, James Babb: "Without

[80]Charles Eberstadt to Earl Vandale, October 31, 1947. Vandale Papers, Nita Stewart Haley Memorial Library. The "marriage certificate" is filed next to the letter cited. J. Evetts Haley's little memoir on Earl Vandale's collecting is one of the best western book collecting reads around: *Earl Vandale on the Trail of Texas Books* (Canyon, Tex.: Palo Duro Press, 1965).

[81]Charles Eberstadt to Earl Vandale, February 4, 1948. Vandale Papers, Nita Stewart Haley Memorial Library.

[82]Earl Vandale to Charles Eberstadt, March 20, 1948. Vandale Papers, Nita Stewart Haley Memorial Library.

any question, this is one of the very great rarities of Western Americana. The only other known file of the superlatively rare volume is in the Colorado Historical Society and I well remember how difficult it was to even get near it out there. They would let you look at it but not touch it and two men stood guard while you were in the vault where it reposed." Edward added humorously, "So, of course, try as I would, I never was able to walk away with it."[83]

In the search for valuable files of western newspapers, the Eberstadts developed a relationship with Malcolm Wyer, head of the Denver Public Library. At one point he solicited their opinions on some duplicate files of newspapers at the library. Wyer had written to the Eberstadts asking if they would be interested in duplicate files of some Central City, Colorado, newspapers from the late 1860s and 1870s in exchange for rare books from their catalogues. Edward wrote back, "I think your suggestion to exchange the newspapers for items from our catalogues is a good one. This is entirely satisfactory to us, and in line with arrangements which we have made with certain other Western libraries, among them your good neighbors the Colorado Historical Society."[84]

When Wyer was asked what he wanted for the duplicates, he responded, "I have had some difficulty in making up my mind what is the best thing for us to do in regard to the file of Central City newspapers."[85] Wyer had thought of gifting the newspapers to another Colorado institution, but then considered that the papers might be more useful to researchers if they were placed in a more distant institution. Also, "I am at a loss to set a price for this file. We have found that except for the Denver papers, we have more occasion to refer to the Central City papers than any other Colorado papers."[86] Ultimately Wyer suggested a trade credit of $1,000 for the newspapers, which the Eberstadts countered with an offer of $600 and only two files of newspapers (the *Central City Daily Miner's Register* and the *Central City Weekly Miner's Register*) instead

---

[83]Edward Eberstadt to James T. Babb, July 13, 1951. Box 26, Manuscripts and Archives, Yale University Library.

[84]Edward Eberstadt to Malcolm Wyer, March 9, 1950. Edward Eberstadt & Sons Records, Denver Public Library.

[85]Malcolm Wyer to Edward Eberstadt, March 11, 1950. Edward Eberstadt & Sons Records, Denver Public Library.

[86]Ibid.

of the four files offered by Wyer. This offer was accepted, and when Lindley visited Denver that summer of 1950, Wyer offered some other duplicates for trade credit, including "a duplicate lot of the Eureka Laws and of the Spanish Bar District Laws, as also a copy of Burris' *Reminiscences*."[87] The *Laws of the Eureka District* (Denver, 1860) is one of only two known items printed by the Rocky Mountain Herald press, and the *Revised Laws of the Spanish Bar District* (Denver, 1861) is equally rare, while the last copy of the Martin Burris, *True Sketches of the Life and Travels* (Salina, Kan., 1910) to appear at auction was in 1958. After the Eberstadts accepted the offer, Wyer took in exchange the Colorado mining archive of R. H. Rickard.

Sometimes the Eberstadts were blamed by a collector for offering too many interesting potential acquisitions. Thomas Streeter was working on a bibliography of Texas imprints to 1845 at this time, but as he wrote to Wagner:

> The other day I got from Eberstadt a beautiful copy of the privately printed Osborne Cross, *A Report in the Form of a Journal* (Philadelphia, 1850) which you featured in the first edition of your *Plains and Rockies*, and I think there is a possibility that before long I will be able to get the Frederick A. Wislizenus, *Ein Ausflug* (St. Louis, 1840) [a rare account of a journey to the Rocky Mountains]. As a matter of fact, I have been indulging in a book buying spree, for as I wrote you a while ago, this is the first time I have had since I have been collecting books that I have really had any money to spend on them and this may well be temporary. One bad feature of all this is that I am so busy buying books and then writing notes about them that not much is being done on the Texas Bibliography.[88]

Eberstadt was certainly happy to be selling books to his dear friend and customer.

Streeter recounted some news about Edward: "I see our mutual friend Eberstadt from time to time. He has been on the water wagon now for some months and is positively exuding virtue. He still knows how to charge for books. This reminds me of the time you bought

---

[87]Edward Eberstadt to Malcolm G. Wyer, July 14, 1950. Edward Eberstadt & Sons Records, Denver Public Library.

[88]Thomas W. Streeter to Henry R. Wagner, April 17, 1943. Box 15, Streeter Papers, American Antiquarian Society. Part of Streeter's newfound wealth was coming from the Ungalik Syndicate, which operated a dredge in Alaska that had amazing returns—one good summer meant a profit of $200,000, which he spent on books.

Ridge's *Joaquin Murieta* from him for $750, which you afterwards were good enough to turn over to me. At the time we both thought Ed had gone pretty far, but after reading Joe Jackson's chapter on Joaquin in Joe's recent *Bad Company*, I think we all did pretty well."[89]

Streeter did more than well with his copy of John Rollin Ridge's *The Life and Adventures of Joaquin Murieta, the Celebrated California Bandit* (San Francisco, 1854). This book is usually known as the "Yellow Bird" because of Ridge's use of that pseudonym. It is the rarest single item in the list of California books compiled by the Zamarano Club, a book collecting club named after California's first printer. When the Yellow Bird came up in the second session of the Streeter Sale on April 20, 1967, Lindley planned to bid up to $5,000 for the rare book, but he wasn't even the underbidder on it; Peter Decker bought it for Frederick Beinecke for $10,000.[90] The only other copy of the Yellow Bird to sell at auction (since Streeter's) sold in 1993 for $69,000; then ten years later that same copy sold for just over $86,000.

One area outside of bookselling that Edward, and later Lindley, cultivated was the field of original western paintings and drawings. The Eberstadts issued two catalogues devoted entirely to western paintings and art: *Catalogue 139 A Distinguished Collection of Western Paintings*, which featured an introduction from western art historian Harold McCracken, and *Catalogue 146 American Paintings— Historical—Genre—Western* was issued as the golden anniversary catalogue of the firm in 1958. Many of these artworks were owned in partnership with two New York dealers who had pioneered dealing in American art—J. N. "Jack" Bartfield and Kennedy Galleries, headed by Rudolph Wunderlich.

It is interesting, therefore, to see an early experience in promoting art to a customer. Edward told Beulah Rollins,

> Some couple of years ago Mr. Coe bought the original painting of Cook landing on the Northwest Coast. This is an enormous painting and one which I cannot plead guilty of having recommended.

---

[89]Thomas W. Streeter to Henry R. Wagner, October 10, 1949. Box 15, Folder 3, Streeter Papers, American Antiquarian Society.

[90]Parke-Bernet Galleries, *The Celebrated Collection of Americana Formed by the Late Thomas Winthrop Streeter*, vol. 2 (New York: Parke-Bernet Galleries, 1967), 898. The Yellow Bird had originally been scheduled for a later session of the Streeter sale but was moved up so that F. W. Beinecke could purchase it and complete his collection of the Zamorano 80 checklist (Beinecke had been in ill health).

Kashnor charged quite a few thousand dollars for it and I was asked whether or not to buy it.[91] Of course, my knowledge of paintings is as meager as my experience with women, and therefore I left the matter entirely to Mr. Coe's own best judgment. Well, it was ordered. When it came, Mr. Coe rang me up and said, "Come on over, Eberstadt." Mohammed went to the mountain. And if for once Mohammed may wax profane, Mohammed caught hell. . . . I would hate to have to bring up that painting again.[92]

Edward continued, though, to try to interest Coe in historical paintings of western scenes. As their catalogues progressed through the 1950s, more and more space was devoted to the artworks. There is some logic to this; as customers find it harder to add to collections, paintings have the virtue of being unique. Nevertheless, it can be difficult to convert a customer who is interested in the documentary research side (manuscripts and books) to become interested in collecting the visual records of the West.

After one such attempt to interest Coe in an original painting by Frank Lynn of Fort Pelly—an outpost of the Hudson Fur Trade Company in the Pacific Northwest—along with paintings of three other forts, Coe wrote: "Now, let me say of the four paintings you sent me, I would under no circumstances be interested in a flat boat painting nor the Fort Pelly painting. The Fort Custer painting is a watercolor and it is very difficult to locate the Fort. The picture looks more like a Long Island Real Estate development. It is also very difficult to locate the Fort in the Fort Steilacoom painting." The paintings had been offered to Coe at prices from $400 to $450 each, but he concluded, "I venture to state if you put these up at auction you would not get $100 a piece."[93]

Edward was successful in getting Coe to purchase at least one painting, Louis Maurer's *Buffalo Bill on Guard*, painted around 1867 and used to illustrate the cover of Edward Eberstadt & Sons' catalogue 126. The price was $900, and one assumes that Coe purchased it because he already owned Buffalo Bill's ranch in Wyoming.

[91]Leon Kashnor was proprietor of the Museum Book Store in London.

[92]Edward Eberstadt to Beulah Rollins, November 12, 1937. Rollins Collection, Princeton University Library.

[93]W. R. Coe to Edward Eberstadt, May 24, 1954, Box 11, Eberstadt Records, Beinecke Library. A description of the Fort Pelly painting can be found in the Eberstadt catalogue 136: 395.

Sometime in 1953 James Babb and Archibald Hanna were beginning to work with Frederick W. Beinecke as a donor for the Yale Library as well as continuing to work with Coe. When Hanna went over Eberstadts' catalogue 132, he selected nearly two hundred items. About forty of the items were underlined in red, and these were to be submitted to Coe for his approval and purchase for the library; another fifteen or so were underlined in blue and were to be submitted to "FWB"—Frederick W. Beinecke—for his approval and purchase.[94] As an additional inducement, Babb also informed Beinecke that the Eberstadts would give a discount of 25 percent "on any or all of these items," which were purchased from catalogue 132.[95]

This process of submitting catalogues to Coe—and the building of his collection at Yale—continued until Coe's passing on March 14, 1955. Coe remained a true friend to Yale. He gave them his famous collection of western Americana and a thousand-volume collection of rare ornithology as well as endowing both a professorship of American history at Yale and the curatorial chair that Hanna accepted.[96]

Coe's passing meant a new focus on Beinecke as a customer, but this was a delicate dance for the Eberstadts. Peter Decker was Beinecke's primary agent, and the Eberstadts were only able to make a sale by having James Babb forward a list to Beinecke for his consideration. Nevertheless, the Eberstadts continued to cultivate Beinecke as a collector and donor to Yale; Charles could report to Babb that "Mr. Beinecke has called and asked to see the following numbers [fourteen items from catalogue 133] . . . and I think we will get a decision on Monday."[97]

The next year (1954) Lindley and Charles continued to court Beinecke, and Charles was able to report to Hanna, "You will be glad to know that Lin had a most agreeable meeting with F. W. yesterday and that he took all of the items from the Alaska catalogue, as well

[94]Among the items submitted for Coe's consideration from Eberstadt catalogue 132 were numbers 4, 134, 316, 419, 549, 618, and 683, among others; for Beinecke's consideration from catalogue 132 were numbers 26, 48, 73, 96, 355, 526, 700, and 715, among others.

[95]James T. Babb to Frederick W. Beinecke, June 2, 1953. Curatorial Files, Beinecke Library.

[96]"William R. Coe, 85, Sportsman, Dead," *New York Times* (March 16, 1955), 30.

[97]Charles Eberstadt to James T. Babb, January 8, 1954. Box 26, Manuscripts and Archives, Yale University Library. From Eberstadt catalogue 133 the items were 124, 237, 250, 251, 444, 446, 566, 611, 612, 646, 667, 678, 740, and 810.

as the Spanish Southwest material that you wanted. He still has not closed on the Mexican War Collection, but reiterated his decision to buy it . . . a big bundle of good news right before the 4th of July and a long, dry summer."[98] The *Alaska and Northwest Catalogue* was a mimeographed typescript in blue wrappers; technically it was Eberstadt catalogue 148, while the Mexican War collection referred to was apparently a typescript-only list (*Edward Eberstadt & Sons Mexican War Collection*) with no Eberstadt catalogue number, which had 854 Mexican War items. Both of these catalogues seem to have been issued with only one customer in mind—F. W. Beinecke.

Charles and Lindley continued to try to cultivate other western art collectors. One important one who, unfortunately, failed to materialize as a customer was Amon G. Carter of Fort Worth. There are letters to Carter from Charles Eberstadt, who began offering paintings in 1953 to the Fort Worth collector, including Alfred Jacob Miller's *The Pipe of Peace* (not purchased), and H. W. Hansen's *The Apache Renegades in Full Retreat* (offered in March of 1954 for $10,000), and, later, three paintings by H. C. Pratt of the U.S. Boundary Commission, but in each case there was a polite response from Carter's secretary, Katrine Deakins, indicating that Carter was primarily interested in works by Remington and Russell.[99]

The Eberstadts had better luck selling western art to another Texan, H. J. Lutcher Stark of Orange, Texas. In 1957 Lindley sold the Starks an archive of 230 original watercolor and oil sketches (including four large oil paintings) of the Canadian West and Pacific Northwest drawn by artist Paul Kane in 1846. This collection is now housed in the Stark Museum of Art, and while the purchase price

---

[98]Charles Eberstadt to Archibald Hanna, June 26, 1959. Curatorial Files, Beinecke Library.

[99]Charles Eberstadt to Amon G. Carter, April 8, 1953; March 16, 1954; Lindley Eberstadt to Katrine Deakins, April 17, 1958. All Box 4, Folder 1, Amon G. Carter Museum of American Art Archives, Fort Worth, Texas. In addition, Lindley Eberstadt also corresponded earlier with Carter's secretary, Katrine Deakins, offering a Tiffany Remington gold vase for $2,500 (September 15, 1953) and a Remington painting set in Texas, *Hasty Entrenchment Drill in the U.S. Army, Captain Febinger's Company of Infantry*, signed Frederic Remington, Camp Eagle Pass, Texas (offered June 4, 1958), both of which were passed. See Box 36, Folder 1, Amon G. Carter Museum of American Art Archives. Later, in April 1972, Mitchell Wilder, director of the Amon Carter Museum, visited Lindley Eberstadt in his New York City office and asked him to send Catlin's North American Indian portfolio to the museum on approval, which the museum purchased in May 1972.

was not disclosed, it was estimated by the *New York Times* to be in excess of $100,000.[100]

Besides being an antiquarian bookseller extraordinaire, Edward had the unusual ability to cultivate sincere friendships, and he took seriously those obligations. He once counseled his lifelong friend and customer, Everette DeGolyer (who had apparently written him in a bit of a forlorn state): "You said you felt lonesome. My friend, on this subject I am an authority. I have never conquered it, but I find that one can live with it, and by forcing the mind to eschew melancholy thoughts and dwell on the trivialities of the day, time wears away and philosophy comes to our aid. Draw on it now. You have many friends—many more than you know of—and each, in his way, hurts at this trouble to you. One of them signs himself affectionately, Ed."[101]

Eberstadt's friends were equally helpful to him. Hanna wrote a letter to cheer up Edward during his convalescence: "I understand from various secret sources that you have now taken so many vitamin pills that you are becoming a menace to every pretty nurse within a hundred yards. . . . All joking aside, I am delighted to hear that you are making such a splendid recovery and hope that we will soon see you back in your old haunt again. For one thing, I need your counsel as adviser to this collection to protect against two dealers, brothers, named Eberstadt who insist on running me into debt."[102]

Edward could not bear a grudge against his old friend Wagner forever, even if the insult had been published in a book. When he heard that Wagner had broken his leg, he wrote Henry wishing him well in 1948. Edward remembered Wagner's first visit to his new store around 1910, writing to him: "What a long ago vista, most of it now tenderly nostalgic, you have evoked by your letter to me. Forty years and more ago! Yes, I remember. How clearly our thousand and one book chats come back; the discussions of Pattie and Palmer and Leonard and all that host of trappers and explorers, who, after all,

[100]"Texan Acquires Sketches of West," *New York Times* (October 27, 1957), 84.

[101]Edward Eberstadt to Everette L. DeGolyer, October 14, 1949. DeGolyer Library. DeGolyer had begun suffering from aplastic anemia (a bone marrow disease) sometime in 1949, which led to the loss of his eyesight; he committed suicide in 1956.

[102]Archibald Hanna to Edward Eberstadt, April 17, 1958. Curatorial Files, Beinecke Library.

have preceded us only by a little while into the limbo of a distant sunset land."[103]

Wagner wrote back to Edward, seemingly glad to have the relations knitted up: "I have occasionally heard about you from Tom Streeter and hope that now you have resumed friendly relations with me that I may hear from you yourself. Your letters were always interesting and I have always been sorry I did not keep a file of them. . . . As I said before, I was more than pleased to receive your kindly letter and hope some day I may get more of them."[104]

Very rarely, a bookseller at the culmination of a distinguished career might receive an invitation to take a position of curator or adviser to a collection. After Coe indicated that the Yale University Library would be receiving his collection, the university librarian, James Babb, invited Edward Eberstadt to be the adviser of the collection for the first three years. Ed wrote the following: "Thank you so much . . . but to appoint a guy whose feet—both of them—are already in the grave to a position of this kind for a tenure of *THREE YEARS* is indeed the height of something or other. Is you all trying to kid me?"[105]

Babb, never one to resist a temptation to joust, replied, "To a person of any intelligence at all it would be perfectly obvious that we appointed you as advisor to the William R. Coe Collection for a period of three years because we felt certain that you would fill only a few days of your tenure. Also, anyone of intelligence would not wish to be saddled with you for three years."[106]

As Edward turned over more of his business to his sons, Lindley began visiting collectors and collections, combining his love of scouting with his passion for angling. Edward wrote, perhaps a bit wistfully, to the librarian at the Denver Public Library about one such visit in the summer of 1950. "I am in a very envious mood today on two counts: 1st, because Lindley had the nice little visit with

---

[103]Edward Eberstadt to Henry R. Wagner, May 9, 1949. Box 1, Wagner Papers, Beinecke Library.

[104]Edward Eberstadt to Henry R. Wagner, January 15, 1948. Box 1, Wagner Papers, Beinecke Library.

[105]Edward Eberstadt to James T. Babb, November, 1943. Box 10, Manuscripts and Archives, Yale University Library.

[106]James T. Babb to Edward Eberstadt, November 11, 1943. Box 10, Eberstadt Records, Beinecke Library.

you this morning, and 2nd—because he is leaving tomorrow for the Gunnison for a week of trout fishing."[107]

Of course, not all rare book activities are business; there is a social side to book collecting as well, and Lindley was justifiably proud to write Babb: "Notification has just been received of my election by the council of the Grolier Club and I must hasten to thank you for your goodness in proposing me for membership. I well realize that your powerful support and that of Mr. Streeter were essential and also that my election is more of a token of respect to Dad than to me. Of course, Jim, this makes us all very happy and I am mighty grateful to you."[108]

Charles, though more well known for his bibliographic research skills, also cultivated long and lasting friendships with customers. To Willis McDonald, a New York attorney who had begun to collect Wyoming books, Charles wrote: "I can't begin to tell you what a pleasure it was for Dad and me to meet you the other day, and have such a long and interesting chat. . . . I hope that you will find some excuse to come on back up here again, as we would love to talk Wyoming books with you."[109] Charles continued Edward's tradition of plying customers with an occasional raised glass of refreshment. He wrote to McDonald: "As one governor said to another, 'It's a long time between drinks.'"[110]

Edward Emory Eberstadt's death on October 2, 1958, aged seventy-five, marked the end of an era in western Americana. The *New York Times* noted that Eberstadt began prospecting for gold in Idaho, California, and British Guiana and had started a Latin American travel magazine before working in rare books for the remainder of his life. "He achieved prominence as a scholar of this nation's early history in the West, was frequently consulted on Western

[107]Edward Eberstadt to Malcolm G. Wyer, July 14, 1950. Edward Eberstadt & Sons Records, Denver Public Library.

[108]Lindley Eberstadt to James T. Babb, February 16, 1954. Box 26, Manuscripts and Archives, Yale University Library.

[109]Charles Eberstadt to Willis McDonald, [undated but spring 1956]. McCracken Research Library, Buffalo Bill Center of the West, Cody, Wy. The McCracken Research Library has over twenty letters from Charles Eberstadt to McDonald (whose collection of Wyoming imprints is there as well).

[110]Charles Eberstadt to Willis McDonald, December 1, 1959. McCracken Research Library, Buffalo Bill Center of the West.

Americana and contributed articles to historical magazines."[111] In contrast to his very public personality, the funeral was private and limited to family.[112]

Just as telling as Edward's influence were the many remembrances from his many friends. In response to a letter of condolence from Everett Graff, Lindley wrote:

> I can't tell you how very much your fine letter about Dad meant to Charles and me. You put your finger on the many wonderful things about him. His accomplishments from scratch (as you say), his winsome quality, but of course Charles and I saw a side of him that no others viewed. As you know he was proud of us but he could be pretty tough too—which was good. Still, I think, no other father was more indulgent of his children than he. So many memories of kindnesses and strange extravagances flood in that I wonder how he could ever tolerate us.[113]

Edward's legacy to his sons was one of the leading rare book firms in the world. Within the next decade after his death, his sons would be among the leading players in the Streeter auction sales of Americana while at the same time witnesses to the winding down of the rare book firm. The legacy and lore of the rare book firm that Edward Eberstadt founded would remain and be carried on by his sons.

---

[111]"Edward Emory Eberstadt Dies at 75; Rare Book Seller, Authority on West," *New York Times* (October 4, 1958), 21.

[112]*AB Bookman's Weekly* (October 20, 1958), 1300.

[113]Lindley Eberstadt to Everett D. Graff, October 12, 1958. Box 3, Folder 9, Graff Papers, Newberry Library.

4

The Pinnacle
and Winding Down
1958 ❧ 1975

The death of Edward was not the end of the Eberstadt rare book firm. Charles and Lindley not only maintained the rare book business but helped it continue to prosper. One important question brought to the fore by Edward's passing concerned their father's legacy. What to do with Edward's extensive correspondence and papers?

Charles, ever the careful historian, wrote to James Babb at Yale:

> As you and Archie have both so often suggested, we have just gone through some of the old files and particularly that portion of them relating to Mr. Coe and his collection. A large carton containing some few thousand letters, a large number of them written by Mr. Coe himself between 1920 and 1955 is on its way to you. Archie has suggested to us several times that we might do a good turn for scholarship if we were to place all our obsolete files in the Yale Library, and suggested that were we to do so, they would be held incommunicado, so to speak, and reference to them would not be made until after Lindley's death and mine.[1]

Charles and Lindley were both concerned that the papers only be used by those who show "Mr. Coe and Dad in a favorable light. There is no need to point out to you that certain debunkers have made

---

[1]Charles Eberstadt to James Babb, May 6, 1959. Box 27, Manuscripts and Archives, Yale University Library.

utter devils out of angels."[2] This concern about Edward's legacy was not misplaced; later the next year, when Edwin Wolf and John F. Fleming's biography of Dr. Rosenbach came out, Lindley wrote to E. J. Beinecke about it: "I found it a fascinating book, though in some respects the revelations seemed to me to violate something of the confidential relationship between buyer and seller. It might be said that Rosenbach kissed, and Wolf and Fleming told."[3]

Archibald Hanna had his own take on the biography of Rosenbach and wrote to Charles: "I suppose the facts which fascinate me are the same ones your father possessed; his immense knowledge and love of books, his wonderfully dramatic flair. It makes me more than ever unhappy that Ed never wrote his autobiography . . . the only thing that would give me greater pleasure would be an inscribed copy of your own memoirs."[4] Unfortunately, neither Charles nor Lindley apparently wrote such a memoir.

One legacy concern of both Charles and Lindley was how to dispose of their father's—and their own—personal rare book collections. Edward had built an incredible collection of Confederate imprints, which he first began collecting in 1910. There may have been a sentimental reason for this collection; Edward's mother, Josephine Caroline Carstarphen, was born in Clark, Alabama, at the beginning of the Civil War in 1861.[5] Eventually the collection amounted to some 500 items, of which 129 were unrecorded imprints, including some remarkable broadsides such as the *Herald Extra* on Valverde, printed in San Antonio (March 16, 1862), giving some of the first news of the Battle of Valverde Pass fought in New Mexico as well as the first broadside from Charleston, South Carolina, announcing *The Union Is Dissolved* (December 20, 1860), among many other important Civil War rarities.

Lindley wrote to Babb pitching the purchase of the Confederate

[2]Charles Eberstadt to James Babb, May 6, 1959. Box 27, Manuscripts and Archives, Yale University Library. Charles wrote again on June 8 that three additional cartons of Coe correspondence were coming (including letters relating to Coe's fight with William F. Buckley and the "pinkies").

[3]Lindley Eberstadt to E. J. Beinecke, December 2, 1960. Box 27, Manuscripts and Archives, Yale University Library.

[4]Archibald Hanna to Charles Eberstadt, November 30, 1960. Box 11, Eberstadt Records, Beinecke Library.

[5]Bernhard Eberstadt and Christof Eberstadt, "The Eberstadt Family Tree," *The Eberstadt Family*, www.eberstadt.info (accessed April 27, 2015).

collection and drew a hand with two crossed fingers in the upper-left margin. Eventually, Yale acquired the collection by giving the Eberstadts $25,000 in duplicates (largely from Coe books, which included some less desirable copies of books donated by Beinecke) and agreeing to pay the remainder of $35,000 out over two years, for a total price of $60,000.[6]

Edward was not the only collector; Lindley collected sporting and fishing books and was a consistent donor over the years of angling books to Yale (as well as constant companion on summer fishing trips with James T. Babb). Lindley sold his angling collection to Yale for $30,000: "I am extremely gratified to learn you are proceeding with the purchase of my private angling collection. I know this has been a project near to your heart for a number of reasons, as it has been to mine. It is good to know that these books will be kept together and that they will be at Yale."[7] Perhaps it did not hurt that both Babb and Lindley were avid sport fishers, and both belonged to the Angling Club in New York City.[8]

Sometimes the legacy concerned a valuable manuscript that the Eberstadts had once handled. Researchers, learning of it, wrote to gain access to it or to find out who owned it. Many of these requests fell into the category of family genealogy, or a historian's research. Certainly one of the most unusual requests in the Eberstadt files, though, involved a priest from the Catholic Church.

Father José del Castillo wrote asking where the Albicuri Manuscript—which related the life of Hernando de Santarén, who had been killed with seven other Jesuits in the Tepehuán Revolt of 1616—had ended up, as he wished to examine it. The Eberstadts' response is similar to many booksellers with a sense of discretion in these circumstances—before bothering a customer (and to weed

---

[6]There were other collections acquired by Yale in these years, including Streeter's Texas collection, for which the Eberstadts were agents; another was a collection of Mexican War manuscripts and materials for $75,000 (which was paid for by F. W. Beinecke).

[7]Lindley Eberstadt to James T. Babb, March 2, 1964. Box 27, Manuscripts and Archives, Yale University Library. Charles offered his collection of philatelic magazines and journals as a gift to Yale, who politely declined and suggested that he sell them with the proceeds to benefit the Yale Library.

[8]After Babb's retirement as Yale librarian on January 31, 1965, he continued as a consultant to the angling collections at Beinecke; the *Times* wryly noted that "his regular assignments will probably involve fishing for gifts to Yale." Harry Gilroy, "Bookman's Hobby Helps Land a Job," *New York Times* (January 30, 1965), 29.

out any kooks), they ask them to outline their reasons for wishing to examine the manuscript in question.

Father Del Castillo responded that the eight Jesuits "shed their blood and gave their lives as martyrs of Christ" and that he had been appointed "Vice Postulant in the cause of the canonization of the eight Jesuits."[9] Lindley gave them the contact information for Yale, which had the manuscript—after all, who are rare booksellers to interfere in the work of God?

Lindley and Charles's concern for their father's legacy was justified. His public reputation for scholarship in western Americana was nowhere more evident than in the desirability of the Eberstadt catalogues. By this time the catalogues had become legendary in their own right as reference works and markers of the rarities of western Americana; even today, the annotation "Not in Eberstadt" carries real cachet for many dealers and collectors.

The value of the catalogues was both because of the scholarship that accompanied each of the bibliographic entries as well as the immense variety of rarities that the Eberstadts handled. The catalogues were also valued for the Eberstadt wit that sometimes appeared unexpectedly. In catalogue 157 (entry 65) Charles could not resist a headline playing on Calamity Jane's real last name (Canary) and wrote, "This Canary is Truly A Rara Avis" (Latin for "Rare Bird"). Hanna, the Coe curator, could not resist replying: "I'm glad to see that your sense of humor has survived the winter, misplaced though it may be. If you had tried to give Calamity Jane the 'bird' to her face you would have soon found out that she could skin more than mules."[10]

Understandably, the firm's customers remained eager to complete their runs of Eberstadt catalogues, but Edward's activities with Anderson Galleries in the early 1920s may also account for the paucity of his own firm's catalogues. In fact, a pencil note at the top of a copy of the Hudson Book Company's catalogue 82 at the American Antiquarian Society states: "Cats 83–90 comprise lots sent to auction," which were probably the Anderson Gallery sales.[11]

---

[9]Father José del Castillo to Lindley Eberstadt, February 21, 1963. Curatorial Files, Beinecke Library.

[10]Archibald Hanna to Charles Eberstadt, May 16, 1961. Curatorial Files, Beinecke Library.

[11]*Hudson Book Company*, catalogue 82. Pencil note on upper cover wrappers, American Antiquarian Society copy. Apparently, this series of catalogues became the auction sale catalogue, *A Great Collection of Original Source Material Relating to the Early West and Far West, November 27–29, 1922* (New York: The Anderson Galleries, 1922).

Earl Vandale, the Texas oil man, began trying to complete a set of the Eberstadt catalogues in the mid-1930s for his reference shelves, and while writing to Charles of his desire to obtain more bibliographies mentioned that "personally I like Eberstadt's catalogues better than anything I've found. This is the reason for my trying to beg you out of some of them."[12] In particular, he wrote to Charles: "Which reminds me that I would like, if you have any extras, some or all of your catalogues. I have Nos. 91, 92, 93, 94, 101 and 102 and I consult them often. I have learned more about books from them than from any bibliographies."[13]

Charles replied to this request of Vandale's: "Am awfully sorry to state that with the exceptions of the catalogues you have, the only ones we have are office copies. You do not say that you have 103 but you probably have—if not, I'll send on a copy. In trying to prepare a complete set for binding, I found that we have no copies at all of about half our catalogues and only one or two of all but the 1929 series and our most recent ones."[14]

Vandale was not the only collector trying to complete his files of the Eberstadt catalogues. When James T. Babb, the head librarian at Yale, realized that the Coe Collection was probably coming to Yale, he wanted a complete file of the catalogues as well: "In our file of book catalogues we have numbers 91–94 and 101 to date of Eberstadt catalogues. I am surprised that we do not have at least a few of the earlier ones, but we did not start systematically keeping them until around 1930."[15]

Lindley responded this way to the request for a complete file: "I am sure that you have all that we have in stock. There was a gap between 94 and 101, during which time several mimeograph lists were attempted, but none of which are on hand. We are likewise out of catalogues prior to 91. In connection with Mr. Coe's books, I am fairly certain that there is a complete set of our catalogues in his library."[16]

---

[12]Earl Vandale to Charles Eberstadt, November 30, 1936. Vandale Papers, Nita Stewart Haley Memorial Library.

[13]Earl Vandale to Charles Eberstadt, March 17, 1936. Vandale Papers, Nita Stewart Haley Memorial Library.

[14]Charles Eberstadt to Earl Vandale, March 27, 1936. Vandale Papers, Nita Stewart Haley Memorial Library.

[15]James T. Babb to Lindley Eberstadt, November 25, 1942. Box 35, Manuscripts and Archives, Yale University Library.

[16]Lindley Eberstadt to James T. Babb, November 27, 1942. Box 35, Manuscripts and Archives, Yale University Library.

The American Antiquarian Society also wished to complete their files of Eberstadt catalogues, which even though sparse, were still much larger than those of others. "We have been checking over our very imperfect files of your book catalogues, and I am in hopes that you can fill in at least part of those we lack."[17]

When Archibald Hanna became curator of western Americana he also wrote to the Eberstadts, wanting to have a complete run of their catalogues for his reference shelf: "In looking over our shelves I find that we have copies of your catalogue numbers 119, 126, 128–132. Undoubtedly Don Wing (Yale curator of literature) has a complete file secreted somewhere in the basement, but I would like them close at hand to consult. If you have copies of any of the numbers we are missing they would be a most welcomed addition to the collection."[18]

In response to the demand from collectors and dealers, Eberstadt catalogues 103–38 (1935–56) were reprinted in 1965 in four volumes as *The Annotated Eberstadt Catalogues of Americana* (Argosy-Antiquarian, 1965). Even though many of the Eberstadt catalogues would not rise to the quality of description that leading rare book dealers are accustomed to providing today, their catalogues are still useful markers of the frequency of books in the trade, and the reprint edition still brings several hundred dollars in today's antiquarian book market. While not a complete collection of their catalogues, with the use of the accessible index volume, it is the next best option for collectors and dealers still interested in bibliographic references for collecting the American West today.

The Eberstadt catalogues' importance extended beyond their bibliographic information to occasionally feature guest introductions by luminaries such as western historians Dale Morgan or J. S. Holliday. In 1963 they invited Archibald Hanna to write an introduction to their catalogue on Texas. The Texas catalogue 162, published in October 1963, elicited widespread congratulations. Senator Ralph W.

---

[17]R. W. G. Vail to Edward Eberstadt, May 21, 1937. Archives, American Antiquarian Society; the AAS library had catalogues 26, 27, 28, 75, 76, 77, 78, 79, 80, 81, 91–94, 101–104, and three with no numbers: "American Local History" (which was received in 1918), "How They Went West," and "When the West Was New." The AAS has since added catalogue 82, which has the infamous ghost entry on the final leaf at number 299 for the Provisional Laws of Jefferson Territory (Omaha, 1860) at $3,000.

[18]Archibald Hanna to Charles Eberstadt, December 2, 1953. Curatorial Files, Beinecke Library.

Yarborough, a longtime Texas book collector, wrote "Congratulations on Catalogue 162 TEXAS. It has more history in it than many conventional Texas histories. It is a service to Texas and to students of the Westward movement on the American Frontier, as well as a credit to you."[19]

Near the time of their last catalogue (168) in 1965, Charles sent Hanna a postcard when it was time to sign some special copies of the catalogue for presentation: "Come early on the 23rd [March] to sign 100 special copies of *The Americana Catalogue*. The honorarium? You will go down in history—down and down and down."[20] Charles was probably alluding to the pile of catalogues that Hanna would need to sign.

In spite of the legendary reputation of the Eberstadt firm and its catalogues, or perhaps in part because of it, Lindley and Charles Eberstadt continued to deal with complaints of high prices for western Americana that had occasionally plagued their father. Charles defended the firm's practices in an article he did for *The Antiquarian Bookman's Yearbook* in 1965:

> Sometimes it is averred that prices of Western books have gone sky high, but this is more apparent than real. . . . The art of establishing fair prices is one of the most difficult that the responsible antiquarian bookman has to master. It is made up of many elements. . . . The dealer must know what other copies have previously appeared, who bought them, at what price, when, who needs the book now, how this copy compares to others for condition, the relationship between this book and others similar which he has handled and a score of other things. Then, taking into consideration his own cost and overhead, applying a certain amount of educated intuition, and tempering the result with a fair amount of conscience, he may hope to arrive at a fairly fair figure.[21]

If Charles's elucidation of the factors in the pricing process seems complicated, that's because it is—but this is still one of the best summaries of what a good antiquarian dealer should take into account when pricing a rare book.

---

[19]Senator Ralph W. Yarborough to the Eberstadts, October 16, 1963. Typed file copy, Curatorial Files, Beinecke Library.

[20]Charles Eberstadt to Archibald Hanna, March 17, 1965. Curatorial Files, Beinecke Library.

[21]Charles Eberstadt, "Western Americana Collecting," reprinted from *Antiquarian Bookman's Yearbook* (1965): 8–10.

Even when offered at trade credit, librarians would still sometimes complain about prices. Apparently Charles and Lindley had listed a Colorado lithographic print by Alfred Mathews, *Mount Silverheels, and Tarryall Gulch*, in their catalogue in the spring of 1961, and it was ordered on approval by Alys Freeze, then head of the Denver Public Library Western History Department.[22] Freeze wrote after receiving the print, "We have decided to keep the Mathews 'Mount Silverheels,' even though I believe at that price it is rank extravagance. I suppose ten years from now that thought will be absorbed with many others."[23] The price of "rank extravagance" in 1961? One hundred dollars.

Lindley and Charles sometimes used Edward's tactics of humor and hyperbole to deflect concern about prices, though not always as successfully as their father. Lindley once wrote asking if Yale had a duplicate copy of the 1835 *Crockett Almanac* that they would be interested in trading for some Eberstadt items. Around this time Hanna had returned a couple of valuable rare books from catalogue 160, and Lindley had complained that "many transactions like this one and we would wind up in the poor-house."[24]

Hanna had been an intelligence officer in the Marines in World War II and could recognize an exaggerated bluff as well as anyone. He responded: "Do let me know in advance when you plan to go bankrupt so I can get there a few days ahead of the sheriff."[25] And in regards to the proposed Crockett duplicate: "Don't just offer me a coon skin cap in trade for the Crockett Almanac when you finally get it."[26]

Of course, once Charles and Lindley were running the business without their father, they could poke fun at themselves as well in regard to pricing: "Lin and I have just joined hands under our séance table and jointly wafted off into a wonderful trance. Whenever the problem of pricing anything comes up we naturally do this together for this way we can see double. Anyway, by somewhat arbitrary standards we have reached a price of $4600 for the Collection of 92

---

[22]Edward Eberstadt & Sons, *Catalogue 156 Americana* (New York, 1961), item 62.

[23]Alys Freeze to Charles Eberstadt, June 16, 1961. Edward Eberstadt & Sons Records, Denver Public Library.

[24]Charles Eberstadt to Archibald Hanna, January 28, 1963. Curatorial Files, Beinecke Library.

[25]Archibald Hanna to Charles Eberstadt, January 30, 1963. Curatorial Files, Beinecke Library.

[26]Ibid.

items of Hawaiiana."[27] Apparently they were not the only antiquarian booksellers to ever consider spiritual pricing; the cost code (used by antiquarian booksellers to record the purchase price of a book with letters in place of numbers from 0 to 9) that the Goodspeed's firm of Boston used was MYPLANCHET—suggesting perhaps the Ouija board nature of pricing.[28]

Charles and Lindley were taking advantage at this time of one of the firm's greatest assets—its established relationship with important collectors. Their understanding of their client's interest sometimes translated into the purchase of an entire catalogue—before any other collector got a crack at it. After Beinecke bought most or all of Eberstadt catalogue 158, *California Delineated*, Charles sent the following postcard to Archibald: "Everett DeGolyer [Jr.] called this morning and said, 'Catalogue 158, items 120, 272, 378 and 380 I don't want, but I'd sure like to have all the others.'"[29] Unfortunately for him, Beinecke had already purchased everything, but this also demonstrates that the Eberstadt catalogues were not being produced entirely for one customer.

One of the most fascinating catalogues issued by the Eberstadts in the early 1960s was catalogue 159, *California Manuscripts*. They enlisted the help of western scholar Dale Morgan, who was working at the Bancroft Library, who not only wrote a nice introduction for the catalogue but also apparently circulated the proof sheets among his fellow librarians and a few collectors too. Charles sent an advance copy of the catalogue to F. W. Beinecke, noting about Morgan, "We had no intention that he should show the copy anywhere, but he has done so and we heard from several quarters over the weekend that California is buzzing! For all the buzzing—needless to say—no one on earth shall have a chance at a single item in this collection until you and Yale have made your selections."[30]

---

[27]Charles Eberstadt to Archibald Hanna, May 14, 1959. Curatorial Files, Beinecke Library.

[28]Cost codes are a ten-letter code, with each letter signifying a number between 0 and 9, used by antiquarian booksellers to record the purchase price; any ten-letter combination of words will work, as long as none of the letters are repeating.

[29]Charles Eberstadt to Archibald Hanna, December 18, 1961. Curatorial Files, Beinecke Library. Everett DeGolyer Jr. had assumed responsibility for continuing the western Americana collection after his father's death.

[30]Charles Eberstadt to Frederick W. Beinecke, March 27, 1962. Box 27, Manuscripts and Archives, Yale University Library.

It was ever thus when a great collector is involved. Frederick Beinecke purchased 55 percent of the collection in catalogue 159 by item count and more than 90 percent by their total value. As Charles wrote, "This is a triumph of both private and institutional collecting."[31]

Even with Beinecke backing many purchases for Yale, sometimes even the Eberstadts' instincts did not come through for them. For example, the *American Constitution* catalogue (166) apparently lacked the Eberstadt golden touch—or should it be said that of a Beinecke? Charles wrote to James Babb with a slight tone of desperation: "Bill Beinecke is having none of the Constitution Catalogue. Any other ideas?"[32] Eventually, though, Beinecke bought nearly $20,000 from the Constitution catalogue.

When catalogue number 161 was almost ready, Charles and Lindley sent the following—slightly over the top—note to Beinecke: "If there is any truth to the parable of the talents (and it comes from a source considered gospel) I think you are going to say, 'Well done, thou good and faithful servants' when you savor the heavenly bouquet wafting from that quintessence of the vintner's art that is Catalogue 161. . . . Not Svengali, nor Merlin, nay, not even Beelzebub himself e'er conjured up such beguiling alchemy as here wrought by Your Good and Faithful Servants, The Wizard Bros."[33] This was not the only catalogue purchase roughly en bloc; from catalogue 161, Yale purchased $83,000 (again paid for by Beinecke).

Besides selling from their own renowned catalogues, as the 1960s progressed the Eberstadts often carried bids to execute on behalf of customers at auction. When the Newberry Library decided to sell their duplicates (from the Everett Graff collection), probably in advance of the Streeter sale, they did it through Parke-Bernet Galleries in New York in the spring of 1966. The Denver Public Library asked Lindley Eberstadt to carry their bids but had little success in the sale, getting only two of their seven bids—number 295, the Charles Siringo, *Two Evil Isms* (Chicago, 1915), for $85, and number 723, A. S. Mercer's promotional work, *Washington Territory: The*

---

[31]It was actually just seven days between the delivery of the proofs on April 12 to F. W. Beinecke and Archibald Hanna and the decision to purchase most of the catalogue.

[32]Charles Eberstadt to James T. Babb, October 5, 1964. Box 27, Manuscripts and Archives, Yale University Library.

[33]Charles and Lindley Eberstadt to Frederick W. Beinecke, April 9, 1963. Curatorial Files, Beinecke Library.

Great Northwest (Utica, N.Y., 1865) for $325, but missing five other rare books from bidding too low.[34]

Thomas W. Streeter's passing on June 12, 1965, meant to the Eberstadts not only the loss of a great friend and customer but the end of an era in Americana collecting. The *New York Times* noted that Streeter had received the Henry R. Wagner Memorial Award from the California Historical Society for his bibliographic contributions, including his *Bibliography of Texas, 1795–1845*. He also received the Gold Medal for distinguished service from the New York Historical Society and served as president of the American Antiquarian Society and the Bibliographical Society of America.[35]

The much anticipated Streeter sale of his collection of Americana was one of the great events in the rare book world at the time, and as a result needed some careful planning and strategizing. As Lawrence C. Wroth, the librarian emeritus of Brown University, wrote in the introduction to the sale catalogues: "Any bookman acquainted even in small degree with the Americana Library of Thomas Winthrop Streeter is aware of three of its features which make it comparable only to the memorable Brinley Collection (dispersed at auction in the years 1879–93). In size, scope and integration of elements it stands with the Brinley and surpasses all other American private libraries."[36] These are some remarkable words about the breadth and depth of the Streeter collection, as the Brinley sale was *the* Americana event of the nineteenth century.[37] An examination of the Brinley sale catalogues shows that nearly 10,000 lots were sold over the

[34]Edward Eberstadt & Sons Invoice, May 6, 1966. Edward Eberstadt & Sons Records, Denver Public Library. The missed books were numbers 32 (Pierre-Jean De Smet, *The Indian Mission*, $300); 107 (Capt. John Palliser, *Exploration—British North America*, $1,500); 392 (George Devol, *Forty Years a Gambler*, $90); 546 (Joseph A. Stuart, *My Roving Life*, $675); and 592 (William R. Broughton, *A Voyage of Discovery*, $950).

[35]"Thomas Winthrop Streeter Dies; Collector of Americana was 81," *New York Times* (June 13, 1965), 85.

[36]Lawrence C. Wroth, "Introduction," *The Celebrated Collection of Americana Formed by the Late Thomas Winthrop Streeter*, vol. 1 (New York: Parke-Bernet Galleries, 1966), i.

[37]Geo. A. Leavitt & Co., *Catalogue of the American Library of the Late Mr. George Brinley of Hartford Conn.* (Hartford: Press of the Case, Lockwood & Brainard Company, 1878–93); Dickinson, *Dictionary of American Book Collectors*, 51–53; William Reese, "George Brinley and His Library," *Gazette of the Grolier Club* 32 (1980), 24–39; Marcus McCorison, "George Brinley, Americanist," *Gazette of the Grolier Club* 32 (1980), 4–23; Kenneth Nebenzahl, "Reflections on the Brinley and Streeter Sales," *Papers of the Bibliographic Society of America* 64 (1970), 165–75.

fourteen years; by comparison, the Streeter sale had nearly 4,500 lots over three years between 1966 and 1969. Interestingly, Brinley left $10,000 to Yale for the purchase of rare books from his sale, and today the Beinecke has over 1,750 items from Brinley's collection.[38]

Since Streeter was a customer of the Eberstadts from the early 1920s, it was only natural that Charles and Lindley—along with Michael Walsh of Goodspeed's in Boston and Roland Tree of Henry Stevens, Son & Stiles, longtime rare book dealers in London and New York— would help organize and select items for the Parke-Bernet Galleries to feature in the sales. Charles reported to Hanna on his meetings with Parke-Bernet Auction Galleries on the organization of the sale: "They really intend to go all out on the catalogues, and I think this will be *the* great sale of the century. Since we won't be too active in the next, I guess we should plan to make the most of it!"[39] Parke-Bernet did go "all out" on the catalogues; the seven-volume set with index remains one of the basic references for rare printed Americana.

Hanna responded, "I am looking forward to this event with mixed awe and trepidation."[40] Hanna's awe was no doubt inspired by the rarity of the items in the forthcoming sale, and his trepidation by the amount of money that would be required to compete for the rarities against other collectors and institutional rare book libraries. Because of the widespread interest in the Streeter sale, many would attend the auction or leave bids with booksellers to execute on their behalf.

The salesroom at Parke-Bernet on the Upper East Side of Manhattan, on Madison between 76th and 77th streets, must have been packed—the *New York Times* reported that the opening session of the sale in the auction room on October 26, 1966, drew over six hundred collectors, dealers, rare book curators, and librarians. Among them were the New York dealer John Fleming (who had trained under Dr. Rosenbach), rare book dealer Kenneth Nebenzahl of Chicago, and Warren Howell of John Howell–Books in San Francisco, curators from rare book collections such as Yale's, the

---

[38]Vincent Giroud, "Modern Books and Manuscripts," Beinecke Rare Book and Manuscript Library, Yale University Library, http://beinecke.library.yale.edu/collections/curatorial-areas/modern-books-and-manuscripts (accessed April 30, 2015).

[39]Charles Eberstadt to Archibald Hanna, January 18, 1966. Curatorial Files, Beinecke Library.

[40]Archibald Hanna to Charles Eberstadt, January 24, 1966. Curatorial Files, Beinecke Library.

John Carter Brown Library at Brown, and Indiana University, and private collectors such as H. Bradley Martin and Henry C. Taylor, who collected the early exploration of the New World.[41]

The Eberstadts carried some smaller bids at this opening sale for the Denver Public Library, among others.[42] However, one dealer dominated the bidding for western Americana—Peter Decker, who was carrying the bids for F. W. Beinecke and won the bidding over and over.[43] Lindley carried seven bids for the Denver Public Library but missed every single one. For example, Lindley bid up to $350 for number 442, a rare Santa Fe, New Mexico, imprint from 1860 dealing with Navajo Indian negotiations, but Peter Decker got it for Beinecke for $3,000—nearly ten times more. For number 500, a very rare *Guide to the Colorado Mines* (San Francisco, 1863), Lindley bid up to $1,500 for Denver, but it sold to Decker (for Beinecke) for $12,000.

As Lindley wrote to the Denver Public Library about the sale, "I am very sorry to report that we had very poor luck at the Streeter Sale. Prices are just through the ceiling. Some things we sold Mr. Streeter a few years ago for $100 or $200 fetched that many thousands. . . . I don't know what the answer is, but money seems to be going out of style, as they say."[44]

Even though Lindley had poor luck bidding for others, there was one book that he did not hesitate to claim for his own. One of the rarest books at this sale was the first book printed west of the Mississippi, the *Laws of the Territory of Louisiana* (St. Louis, 1808), which Lindley jumped in and purchased for $8,000, without carrying a bid for anyone else. After the sale, Lindley wrote to Frederick W. Beinecke about this book,

> I was disappointed that you did not acquire the other most important item at the sale . . . the first book printed west of the Mississippi River and of vital importance as the first laws governing the Louisiana Territory. When Peter [Decker] dropped out of the bidding it was taken

[41]Sanka Knox, "Account of Magellan's Voyage Is Sold for $56,000," *New York Times* (October 26, 1966), 41.

[42]Archibald Hanna to Lindley Eberstadt, October 30, 1967: "We appreciate your efforts. With so little money to work with, we were able to acquire so many important things due only to your superior knowledge and judgment." Curatorial Files, Beinecke Library.

[43]Dickinson, *Dictionary of American Antiquarian Bookdealers*, 48.

[44]Lindley Eberstadt to Alys Freeze, October 28, 1966. Edward Eberstadt & Sons Records, Denver Public Library. The Streeter sale items were numbers 442, 458, 475, 490, 500, 509 and 527.

up by several other contenders, and when I saw he wasn't going on I entered the fracas and carried off the prize at $8,000. I believe this to be the utmost significance to you and the Yale Library as one of the very cornerstones of the collection and will be happy to hold it for you should you care to have it.[45]

This was quite a brave move on Lindley's part, but Beinecke evidently passed on the opportunity, and the Yale collection does not have the book to this day.

The Streeter sale, part IV (April 23–24, 1968), contained the most desirable of all the rare books for western collectors, with sections on the Dakotas, Colorado and the Rockies, Wyoming, Montana, Nevada, the Mormons and Utah, the cattle trade, and the California Gold Rush. Lindley knew that Frederick W. Beinecke was laid up in the hospital, but he wrote to the new director of the Beinecke Library at Yale (Herman W. "Fritz" Liebert):

> This Streeter Sale contains so many key books that escaped the capacious maws of F. W. and Coe that it seems to me this is an opportunity that will not again be vouchsafed in your or in our or perhaps in any lifetime. . . . Of course, it would be a miserable business to burden F. W. with this matter in the hospital, but if presented in the proper light to Bill Beinecke [Frederick's son] and perhaps even to E. J., though I understand he has just made a princely contribution to your funds . . . I would be willing to represent you on a reduced or even no-commission basis. Let me assure you, Fritz, that important books are here that we will not again see.[46]

Apparently Peter Decker kept bidding for Beinecke, since after the sale Lindley wrote: "We got quite a few items though I must say I was disappointed in not getting any of the really star items, but Pete got quite a few so that should make up for quite a lot."[47]

When part V of the Streeter sale came around (October 22–23, 1968), there was one book that Yale particularly wanted—the final Nez Perce Mission imprint, which Coe had never acquired. Lindley took no chances on losing this little book in the sale; he went to the Coe Foundation and secured approval from them for a winning bid.

---

[45]Lindley Eberstadt to Frederick W. Beinecke, October 27, 1967. Curatorial Files, Beinecke Library.

[46]Lindley Eberstadt to Herman Liebert, April 10, 1968. Curatorial Files, Beinecke Library.

[47]Lindley Eberstadt to Archibald Hanna, April 30, 1968. Curatorial Files, Beinecke Library.

Lindley had approval from the foundation and was ready to go to $8,000 to get the Nez Perce imprint; fortunately he only had to pay $3,500. After the sale Lindley wrote to Hanna, "I know you were delighted at the acquisition of the Lapwai Laws." As Lindley noted, this missing Lapwai imprint completed the collecting triumph that Mr. Coe had set out to achieve decades earlier.[48]

When part VI of the Streeter sale came around (April 22–23, 1969), Hanna as the Coe curator was especially interested in two items, number 3374 (a report on the massacre of immigrants near Fort Boise in 1854) and 3388 (a report of the Oregon Mounted Militia in the Modoc War of 1873–74): "I'll see you Tuesday evening at the sale in the vain hope that there will be no competition."[49] Such is the hope of every aspiring purchaser at every antiquarian auction. Unfortunately, the report of the massacre went to Leona Rostenberg for $1,200, but Lindley seems to have been successful in obtaining the Oregon Modoc Report for Yale for $1,200.

Sometime after the Streeter sale, the Eberstadt brothers began to contemplate a life outside the rare book business. The firm's last catalogue was number 168 (issued on September 21, 1965), though they had had a couple of auction sales, but now Hanna wrote to them after a visit: "The only thing that bothered me was the conversation about the future dissolution of the business. . . . I am not psychologically resigned to the fact that even in the distant future there should come a day when there is no Edward Eberstadt & Sons. Fortunately, two gorgeous reprobates like you are likely to outlive a saintly character like myself."[50]

As part of the winding-down process of their rare book firm, the Eberstadts had courted several institutions about the purchase of their inventory, but the most promising opportunity seemed to be one with the University of Texas in 1971. Interestingly, the lead player in this deal was Everett L. DeGolyer Jr., whose father had been one of Edward Eberstadt's earliest customers back in the 1920s.

Everett DeGolyer Jr. lived in Dallas, but the DeGolyer Foundation had not yet chosen a permanent home for the western book

---

[48]Lindley Eberstadt to Archibald Hanna, October 28, 1968. Curatorial Files, Beinecke Library.

[49]Archibald Hanna to Lindley Eberstadt, April 17, 1969. Curatorial Files, Beinecke Library.

[50]Archibald Hanna to Lindley and Charles Eberstadt, May 21, 1968. Curatorial Files, Beinecke Library.

collection—the choice was between the University of Texas and Southern Methodist University in Dallas. DeGolyer Jr. reported to the foundation's board in May 1972 "that since July of 1971 until May of this year he had worked on behalf of the University of Texas system, at his own expense, to acquire the Eberstadt collection of books at a cost of around five million dollars."[51] This would have been an amazing coup for the University of Texas, but the deal fell through in late April 1972.

Even though the University of Texas deal fell through, DeGolyer Jr. decided to take advantage of the negotiations to acquire some choice rarities for the foundation library. Lindley wrote to him, "I can't tell you how good it was to see you when you were up here and to have concluded such a favorable piece of business as well."[52] Even though the Eberstadts had been winding down some rare book business affairs, Lindley told Everett that he had purchased a rare Luke Tierney guide to the Pike's Peak Gold Rush at a Sotheby's sale earlier that year with Warren Howell of San Francisco for $4,000, so he offered the guide to Everett for $5,000, which was still $2,000 less than the Streeter sale price several years earlier.

Lindley and DeGolyer had also discussed a larger deal where the DeGolyer Foundation would acquire some of the rarest Wagner-Camp titles for $100,000; now Lindley wanted to firm the deal up on paper. "Now, Ev, as you know both Charlie and I are in such bum shape that I think for your and our mutual benefit a statement of terms from you might be advisable. It is my understanding from our discussions that you have decided to purchase up to $100,000 worth of material, payable over five years with 4% interest per annum accruing to the unpaid balance," with the option to add another $100,000 in rare books under the same terms.[53] Lindley was grateful to see some of their rarest books go to one of their oldest customers—who, like the booksellers, had actively continued into the second generation: "With many, many thanks for this great stroke for the Eberstadts, and I am firmly convinced for the DeGolyers as well, I remain, as ever, very sincerely yours."[54]

Eventually this deal netted the DeGolyer Library one hundred

---

[51]DeGolyer Foundation Minutes, May 31, 1972. DeGolyer Library.
[52]Lindley Eberstadt to Everett DeGolyer Jr., May 1, 1972. DeGolyer Library.
[53]Ibid.
[54]Ibid.

rare Wagner-Camp items, plus a variety of other research materials, for $100,000. In spite of the importance of this acquisition, the foundation board evidently balked at such a large expenditure without prior approval.[55] Among the rarities acquired were a long run of the *Deseret News* (first newspaper in Utah Territory), including the entire first year; D. P. Whiting's *Army Portfolio* (New York, 1847) with hand-colored lithographic views of the Mexican-American War; Alfred E. Mathews, *Gems of Rocky Mountain Scenery* (New York, 1869); and Henry J. Warre, *Sketches in North America and the Oregon Territory* (London, 1848), a set of beautiful hand-colored lithograph views of Oregon and the Northwest, among many other rarities.

After the receipt of many of the rarities, Everett was feeling a little overwhelmed in his office surrounded by the treasures. He wrote to Lindley, "The material all arrived here in excellent condition. I was somewhat terrified at the thought of all that dollar value causally sitting on my office floor, so my first thought was to send it out to the library in a Wells Fargo armored truck. However, they only work on contract, so we finally settled for another lesser firm with gun-toting employees."[56] One only wonders how this might have fueled a New York bookman's perception of Texas book people, but Lindley was game: "Your experience with Wells Fargo and gun-slingers struck a responsive chord here."[57]

Some of the camaraderie felt by Everett DeGolyer Jr. and the Eberstadts is seen after this last deal. Everett wrote later: "One thought that should have been expressed is that we have conspicuously been patsies for the good wares offered by the firm of Edward Eberstadt and Sons and now to the second generation! While not a Papist by inheritance or persuasion, I wish you were like Rome and could go on forever."[58]

Lindley responded with these words: "I appreciate your thought regarding Rome and eternal existence. I may say that my father was born a Catholic but left the fold as soon as he was able to toddle, and I have had no inclination to sign on."[59] Then, just to ensure he

---

[55]DeGolyer Foundation Minutes, May 31, 1972. DeGolyer Library. The motion to approve the purchase was made by that savvy bookman, Decherd Turner, who later directed the Bridwell Library at SMU and the Ransom Center in Austin.

[56]Everett DeGolyer Jr. to Lindley Eberstadt, May 8, 1972. DeGolyer Library.

[57]Lindley Eberstadt to Everett DeGolyer Jr., May 10, 1972. DeGolyer Library.

[58]Everett DeGolyer Jr. to Lindley Eberstadt, May 8, 1972. DeGolyer Library.

[59]Lindley Eberstadt to Everett DeGolyer Jr., May 10, 1972. DeGolyer Library.

was not misunderstood, Lindley added: "I'm not doing anything to extend my lifespan at the moment, and couldn't care less."[60]

Lindley not only maintained professional relationships with the firm's established clients, but he continued his father's tradition of cultivating warm friendships with them as well. Although Hanna regarded all the Eberstadt family with fondness, he came to be closest to Lindley. After one poignant visit in 1972 he wrote,

> As has so often happened in the last twenty years, I came home last night in a very sentimental mood, and you know how distressing that is for a New Englander. . . . I was thinking of what we have been building here at Yale over all these years and what a tremendous part you have played in it. Of course, many others have had a hand in this, including your father and Charles, but it has always been you that I have worked with most closely. I suppose it was because I always knew that when I came to you I would find not only expert advice, but also joyful enthusiasm for what we were trying to do. Laying aside all modesty, I will say that together we have created something that no one will ever be able to duplicate.[61]

Later Hanna tried to get Lindley to travel with him on one his western jaunts to visit booksellers: "I do wish you were coming with us this summer. Our all too brief visits together never seem to get the affairs of the world settled, but if we had ten thousand miles for the conversation to spread out over, just imagine the possibilities. Going over the Rockies and the Sierras we could engage in the loftiest of discourse; while crossing Nevada and Utah we could turn to politics and produce a conversation as arid and sterile as the surroundings themselves."[62]

There were a number of factors that influenced the end of Edward Eberstadt & Sons. Certainly the brothers' drinking habits and declining health were important issues. Lindley's wife, Clarissa, was said to be his main restraint on drinking, but her death in 1971, after nearly thirty-four years of marriage, affected Lindley deeply. Everett DeGolyer Jr. recalled drinking so much late into the night with the brothers after one of his visits in the early 1970s that the only way he could get down the stairs at 888 Madison was to "bump

---

[60]Ibid.

[61]Archibald Hanna to Lindley Eberstadt, April 26, 1972. Curatorial Files, Beinecke Library.

[62]Archibald Hanna to Lindley Eberstadt, June 25, 1973. Curatorial Files, Beinecke Library.

down on his butt." Additionally, both Lindley and Charles had moved to New Jersey, and the daily commute to Manhattan took its toll on their aging bodies. So to be closer to home, in January 1973 the Eberstadts moved their business headquarters from 888 Madison Avenue (where they had worked since the early 1950s) to Montclair, New Jersey.[63] The brothers were certainly aware of their own encroaching mortality, and part of this move may have been a reflection of the change in business for them.

Another contributing factor that affected the firm's reluctance to issue catalogues and sell books was that by this time, the cost value of the inventory had been written down to zero, so that each book sold was pure profit and taxed accordingly at the then-prevalent higher tax rates. Then Charles, who had contributed so much bibliographic knowledge to the firm, was diagnosed with cancer and finally succumbed on June 29, 1974.[64] The death of Charles meant that the vast rare book inventory needed to be dealt with for estate tax purposes. Complicating the estate tax issue was the difficult personal relationship between Lindley and Charles's wife. For all those reasons, the firm needed to sell its inventory to one buyer and not one book at a time.[65]

One potential purchaser was Kenneth Nebenzahl and Warren Howell, rare book dealers of Chicago and San Francisco, who were interested in purchasing the firm's inventory but balked at Lindley's asking price for the collection of around $3.25 million—though, of course, significantly less than the $5 million price for the University of Texas.[66] At this point, a young ambitious bookseller from Austin, Texas—John H. Jenkins Jr.—stepped up, tapping an old college friend, Robert Venable, a Dallas oil man who had access to the Allen family of investment bankers.[67]

---

[63]888 Madison Avenue is on the west side of Madison Avenue near the corner of 72nd Street. They moved to 70 Park Street, Montclair, N.J.

[64]*New York Times* (June 30, 1974), 30.

[65]Personal conversation with William Reese, April 28, 2015.

[66]William Reese is the source of the $3.25 million purchase price; Calvin Trillin, in *Trillin on Texas* (Austin: University of Texas Press, 2011), 66, says that it was $2.7 million.

[67]John H. Jenkins Jr., "The Eberstadt Caper," in *Audubon and Other Capers: Confessions of a Texas Bookmaker* (Austin: Pemberton Press, 1975), 105–20. When Howell and Nebenzahl learned that an offer to buy at the asking price had been made, they countered with a higher offer that, according to Jenkins, was $250,000 more. But working with investment bankers and many attorneys meant that the purchase offer was iron-clad with no escape clause for the Eberstadts, even with a higher offer from another party.

The story of Edward Eberstadt & Sons largely ends with the sale of their inventory to John H. Jenkins Jr. in 1975. The *New York Times* reported: "It cost John H. Jenkins of Texas several million dollars to perform what he called a 'cultural shift to the Southwest.' Mr. Jenkins, who is a 35 year old bespectacled bibliophile, rare book dealer and publisher, has bought the rare book and manuscript collection of Edward Eberstadt & Sons." Of course, following those books and Johnny Jenkins's flamboyant career after that is the subject of another book.[68]

The Eberstadt era finally ended with Lindley's passing in October 1984 and the sale of his personal collection of rare western books by Sotheby's on May 1, 1985. Charles's personal western Americana collection had been sold anonymously at Sotheby's on April 28, 1982.

How to account for the widespread collecting interest in the American West that Edward Eberstadt & Sons helped develop? Earlier in 1958, Lewis Nichols of the *New York Times* speculated on this interest in collecting the West, elaborating on the famous Jimmy Walker saying that besides New York having more Italians than Rome, more Jews than Jerusalem, and more Irish than Dublin, it now had more cowboys than Cheyenne. Nichols quoted Harold McCracken, whose book on western artist Frederic Remington (out since 1948) had sold 20 percent better in 1957 than the year before, and in 1958 had already outsold the numbers for 1957. Nichols then asked Charles Eberstadt, who replied, "There is more fine Western Americana in the East than anywhere else. People want something different—not the skyscrapers they see all around them, but shooting, cowboys, landscape. The west is less than 100 years old, and . . . only in the last fifty have we begun to appreciate Western history." When Nichols asked Charles which book he thought most influential for developing the interest in western collecting, he proposed Bernard DeVoto's *Across the Wide Missouri*, and Peter Decker attributed some of the western collecting interest to an early exposure to Owen Wister's famous western novel, *The Virginian* (1902).[69] In

[68]*New York Times* (August 21, 1975); see also John H. Jenkins Jr., *Audubon and Other Capers* (Austin: Pemberton Press, 1975); Calvin Trillin, "Knowing Johnny Jenkins," *New Yorker*, October 30, 1989, 79–97; and Thomas W. Taylor, *Texfake: An Account of the Theft and Forgery of Early Texas Printed Documents* (Austin: W. Thomas Taylor, 1991).

[69]Lewis Nichols, "In and Out of Books," *New York Times Book Review* (January 12, 1958), 8.

addition to the contribution of popular history and literature about the West, certainly some of the credit for the interest of at least two earlier collectors (Coe and Voorhis) came from the collectors' own experience of owning ranches in the West.

William R. Coe was Edward Eberstadt & Sons' most important customer for more than thirty years; how did he feel about his relationship with the firm? Sometime in 1953 he wrote to Edward, "But for Bishop Thomas introducing you to me, and our long association, there would have been no collection of Western Americana donated by me to the Yale University Library. You have rendered wonderful assistance which enabled me to derive a great deal of satisfaction and pleasure in assembling the collection, which I appreciate most highly."[70]

Edward, Lindley, and Charles Eberstadt left a legacy of having created and built one of the most important rare book firms in the field of western Americana, at a time when the West itself was still in the process of being settled. The passion of Edward, and later Lindley and Charles, for building collections of western history meant that these rare books and manuscripts found homes in institutions such as the Beinecke Library (Yale), Princeton University, the Newberry Library (Chicago), the Bancroft Library (Berkeley), the Huntington Library (San Marino, Calif.), the American Antiquarian Society library (Worcester, Mass.), the J. Evetts Haley Memorial Library (Midland, Tex.), the Buffalo Bill History Library (Cody, Wy.), and the DeGolyer Library (Dallas), among many others.

The Eberstadts though their catalogues, publications, and scholarship contributed significantly to nearly every great collection of western American printed and manuscript materials that are still consulted by scholars, historians, and collectors today. The Eberstadt legend continues when their catalogues and publications are consulted for their bibliographic and historic notes by curators, dealers, and collectors; the legacy is most visible when these original materials are used to tell and retell the life, history, and culture of the American West.

---

[70] Edward Eberstadt to James T. Babb, January, 1953. Box 26, Manuscripts and Archives, Yale University Library.

Bibliography

ARCHIVAL SOURCES

American Antiquarian Society Archives. American Antiquarian Society, Worcester, Massachusetts.

Amon G. Carter Museum of American Art Archives. Amon Carter Museum, Fort Worth, Texas.

Curatorial Files of Western Americana. Beinecke Library, Yale University, New Haven, Connecticut.

DeGolyer, Everette L. Papers. DeGolyer Library, Southern Methodist University, Dallas, Texas.

Eberstadt, Edward, & Sons. Records. Beinecke Library, Yale University, New Haven, Connecticut.

Eberstadt, Edward, & Sons. Records. Western History and Genealogy, Denver Public Library, Denver, Colorado.

Graff, Edward D. Papers. Newberry Library, Chicago, Illinois.

Heaston, Michael D. Collection of Eberstadt Materials. Wichita, Kansas.

McDonald, Willis. Papers. McCracken Research Library, Buffalo Bill Center of the West, Cody, Wyoming.

Reese, William. Private Collection, New Haven, Connecticut.

Rollins, Philip Ashton. Collection. Department of Rare Books and Special Collections, Princeton University Library, Princeton, New Jersey.

Streeter, Thomas W. Papers. American Antiquarian Society, Worcester, Massachusetts.

University Library Records. Manuscripts and Archives. Yale University Library, Yale University, New Haven, Connecticut.

Vandale, Earl. Papers. J. Evetts Haley Collection, Nita Stewart Haley Memorial Library, Midland, Texas.

Voorhis, Charles B. Archive. Collection of William Reese, New Haven, Connecticut.

Wagner, Henry Raup. Papers. Beinecke Library, Yale University, New Haven, Connecticut.

Printed Sources

Adams, Thomas R. "Lathrop Colgate Harper, 1867–1950." *Gazette of the Grolier Club* 26/27 (1977): 3–22.

Anderson Galleries. *A Great Collection of Original Source Material Relating to the Early West and the Far West.* New York: n.p., 1922.

Anonymous. ["Purchase of Eberstadt Stock."] *New York Times* (August 21, 1975).

Axe, Ruth Frey. "Henry R. Wagner: An Intimate Profile." *AB Bookman's Yearbook.* Clifton, N.J.: AB Bookman, 1979.

Bentley, Esther Felt. "A Conversation with Mr. Rollins." *Princeton University Library Chronicle* (June 1948): 178–90.

Blew, John. *The Lives and Work of Wright and Zoe Howes and the Story of U.S.iana.* Chicago: Privately printed, 2014.

Brooks, Philip. "Notes on Rare Books." *New York Times* (November 9, 1941).

———. "Notes on Rare Books." *New York Times* (February 21, 1943).

Camp, Charles L., ed. *Henry R. Wagner's The Plains and the Rockies: A Bibliography of Original Narratives of Travel and Adventure, 1800–1865.* Columbus, Ohio: Long's College Book Company, 1953.

Clark, Robert A. *The Arthur H. Clark Company: A Bibliography and History, 1902–1992.* Spokane, Wash.: Arthur H. Clark, 1993.

Dickinson, Donald C. *Dictionary of American Antiquarian Booksellers.* Westport, Conn.: Greenwood Press, 1998.

———. *Dictionary of American Book Collectors.* Westport, Conn.: Greenwood Press, 1986.

Dobbs, Harold W. "Philip Ashton Rollins, '89." *Princeton University Library Chronicle* 9 (June 1948): 177.

Drury, Clifford M. "Reminiscences of a Historian." *Western Historical Quarterly* 5, no. 2 (April 1974): 143.

Dykes, Jeff. "A Personal Memoir about Edward Eberstadt." *AB Bookman's Weekly* (October 7, 1958), 2512–13.

Eberstadt, Charles. "Western Americana Collecting." *Antiquarian Bookman's Yearbook* (1965): 8–10.

Eberstadt, Edward. "The Journal of Riley Root." *California Historical Quarterly* 10, no. 4 (December 1931): 396–405.

———. "The Thomas W. Streeter Collection." *Yale Library Gazette* 31 (April 1957): 147–53.

———. "The William Robertson Coe Collection of Western Americana." *Yale Library Gazette* 23 (October 1948): 1–130.

Everitt, Charles. *Adventures of a Treasure Hunter: A Rare Bookman in Search of American History.* Boston: Little, Brown, 1951.

Gilroy, Harry. "Bookman's Hobby Helps Land a Job." *New York Times* (January 30, 1965), 29.

Haley, J. Evetts. *Earl Vandale on the Trail of Texas Books.* Canyon, Tex.: Panhandle Plains Museum, 1965.

Hanna, Archibald. "Frederick W. Beinecke, 1887–1971." *Yale Library Gazette* 45 (October 1971): 65–66.

Harding, George L. "A Census of California Spanish Imprints, 1833–1845." *California Historical Quarterly* 12 (June 1933): 125–36.

———. "In Memoriam, Edward Emory Eberstadt." *California Historical Quarterly* 37, no. 4 (December 1958): 375.

Heartman, Charles F. "Lathrop Colgate Harper." *The American Collector* 1 (January 1926): 139–43.

Hogarth, Georgina, ed. *The Letters of Charles Dickens, Vol. 2, 1857–1870.* London: Oxford University Press, 2002.

Howes, Wright. *U.S.iana, 1650–1950: A Selective Bibliography in Which Are Described 11,620 Uncommon and Significant Books Relating to the Continental Portion of the United States.* Rev. ed. New York: R. R. Bowker for the Newberry Library, 1962.

Jenkins, John H., Jr. "The Eberstadt Caper," in *Audubon and Other Capers: Confessions of a Texas Bookmaker,* 105–20. Austin: Pemberton Press, 1975.

Levitt, George A., & Co. *Catalogue of the American Library of the Late Mr. George Brinley of Hartford, Conn.* Hartford, Conn.: Press of the Case, Lockwood & Brainard Co., 1878–93.

Liebert, Herbert W., and Thomas E. Marston. "The Edwin J. Beinecke Memorial Collection." *Yale Library Gazette* 44 (October 1970): 37–52.

Magee, David. "The W. J. Holliday Sale of Western Americana." *Quarterly Newsletter of the Book Club of California* 19 (Summer 1954): 60–64.

Malkin, Sol M. "Obituary of Edward Emory Eberstadt." *AB Bookman's Weekly* (October 20, 1958), 1300.

McCorison, Marcus. "George Brinley, Americanist." *Gazette of the Grolier Club* 32 (1980): 4–23.

Nebenzahl, Kenneth. "Reflections on the Brinley and Streeter Sales." *Papers of the Bibliographical Society of America* 64 (1970): 165–75.

Nichols, Lewis. "In and Out of Books." *New York Times Book Review* (January 12, 1958), 8.

Parke-Bernet Galleries, Inc. *The Celebrated Collection of Americana Formed by the Late Thomas Winthrop Streeter.* New York, 1966–70.

————. *Western Americana, Many of Great Rarity. The Distinguished Collection Formed by W. J. Holliday.* New York, 1954.

Reese, William. "Americana Booksellers." *The 1993 Pforzheimer Lecture of New York Public Library*, March 30, 1993, www.reeseco.com/pforz/htm (accessed August 6, 2014).

Reese, William. *Catalogue 128. The Streeter Sale Revisited.* New Haven, Conn.: William Reese, 1993.

————. *Catalogue 257. The Streeter Sale Revisited.* New Haven, Conn.: William Reese, 2007.

————. "George Brinley and His Library." *Gazette of the Grolier Club* 32 (1980): 24–39.

————. "Pioneering in Western Americana." *AB Bookman's Yearbook.* Clifton, N.J.: AB Bookman, 1985.

————. "Winnowers of the Past: The Americanist Tradition in the Nineteenth Century." Honor's thesis, Yale University, 1977.

————, ed. *Peter Decker's Catalogues of Americana.* Austin: William Reese, 1979.

Rollins, Philip Ashton. *Across the Plains in the Days of the Most Costly Overland Narratives (With Map of the Trail).* New Haven: Overland Press, 1978.

Schaffer, Ellen. "Reminiscences of a California Collector: Mrs. Edward Doheny, 1875–1958." *Book Collector* 14 (Spring 1965): 49–59.

Skiff, Frederick W. *Adventures in Americana: Recollections of Forty Years of Collecting Books, Furniture, China, Guns and Glass.* New York: Metropolitan Press, 1935.

Storm, Colton. *A Catalogue of the Everett D. Graff Collection of Western Americana.* Chicago: Published for the Newberry Library by the University of Chicago Press, 1968.

Streeter, Frank. "Some Recollections of Thomas W. Streeter and his Collecting." *Gazette of the Grolier Club* 32 (1980): 40–50.

Streeter, Thomas W. "Henry R. Wagner: Collector, Bibliographer, Cartographer, Historian." *California Historical Society* 36 (June 1957): 165–75.

————. "The Rollins Collection of Western Americana." *Princeton University Library Chronicle* 9 (June 1948): 191–204.

Taylor, Thomas W. *Texfake: An Account of the Theft and Forgery of Early Texas Printed Documents.* Austin: W. Thomas Taylor, 1991.

Trillin, Calvin. "Knowing Johnny Jenkins." *New Yorker* (October 30, 1989), 79–97.

————. *Trillin on Texas.* Austin: University of Texas Press, 2011.

Vinson, Michael. "New Ranges for Collecting Western Americana: Is It Time to Put the Old Bibliographies Out to Pasture?" *Rare Books and Manuscripts Librarianship* (Spring 1995): 87–93.

———. "Western Americana at Auction." *AB Bookman's Weekly* (October 5, 1992), 1138–39.

Wagner, Henry R. *Bullion to Books: Fifty Years of Business and Pleasure.* Los Angeles: Zamarano Club, 1942.

———. "Recollections of Templeton Crocker." *California Historical Society Quarterly* 28 (December 1949): 363–66.

Wroth, Lawrence C. "Lathrop Colgate Harper: A Happy Memory." *Papers of the Bibliographical Society of America* 52 (1958): 161–72.

Index

E.E.&S., E.E., C.E., and L.E. indicate
Edward Eberstadt & Sons, Edward Eberstadt,
Charles Eberstadt, and Lindley Eberstadt.